CONTENTS

Written by Richard Marson

BBC

Blue Peter

Annual 2008

Pedigree®

Published by Pedigree Books Limited, Beach Hill House, Walnut Gardens, Exeter, Devon, EX4 4DH.
Email: books @pedigreegroup.co.uk By arrangement with the BBC.

£7.99

HELLO THERE!

And a warm welcome to our 37th Blue Peter book. We've tried to fit in all the very best moments from the last year, so see how many of your favourites we've included. As ever, it's been so busy that there's hardly been the chance to catch our breath but then again, that's how we like it. If you're puzzled by what's behind the pictures on this page, check the back of this book for the solutions.

This was Andy's first full year on the programme and when we found out that he couldn't drive, we knew that getting behind the wheel would be one of his earliest challenges. Of course, it wouldn't be Blue Peter without us raising the bar a bit, as you can see on page 84.

Hot on Andy's heels was a certain golden retriever puppy. Magic has certainly lived up to her name and we are keeping our fingers crossed that she'll pass her advanced training and become a working guide dog by the end of 2007. Keep watching to find out.

Our ShoeBiz Appeal was a particular highlight of the year. It is amazing that the orphans of Malawi can find any way of dealing with the horror and tragedy that AIDS has brought to their beautiful country. The fact that, thanks to your efforts, many more will be given help and support is a real credit to the generosity and understanding of Blue Peter viewers everywhere.

This will be Konnie's last year on Blue Peter, having presented nearly 1000 programmes and over 400 films, as well as appearing in ten different annuals. The fact

that she has spent just over a decade with us makes her a Blue Peter record breaker - our longest serving female presenter. Like everyone who really loves the programme, she knows that it will be a wrench to say goodbye.

2008 will be a very important year for us as Blue Peter goes gold and we reach our 50th birthday. We're planning all kinds of celebrations and we hope you're going to join in them. Watching and taking part in the programme has been an experience now shared by generations of grand-parents, parents and children. We think that is something very special.

Zöe Andy Gett Karine xxx

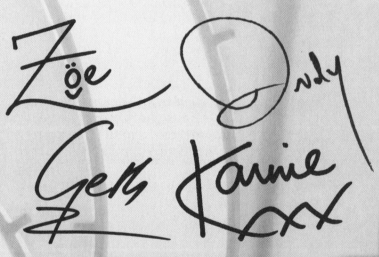

HAVE A

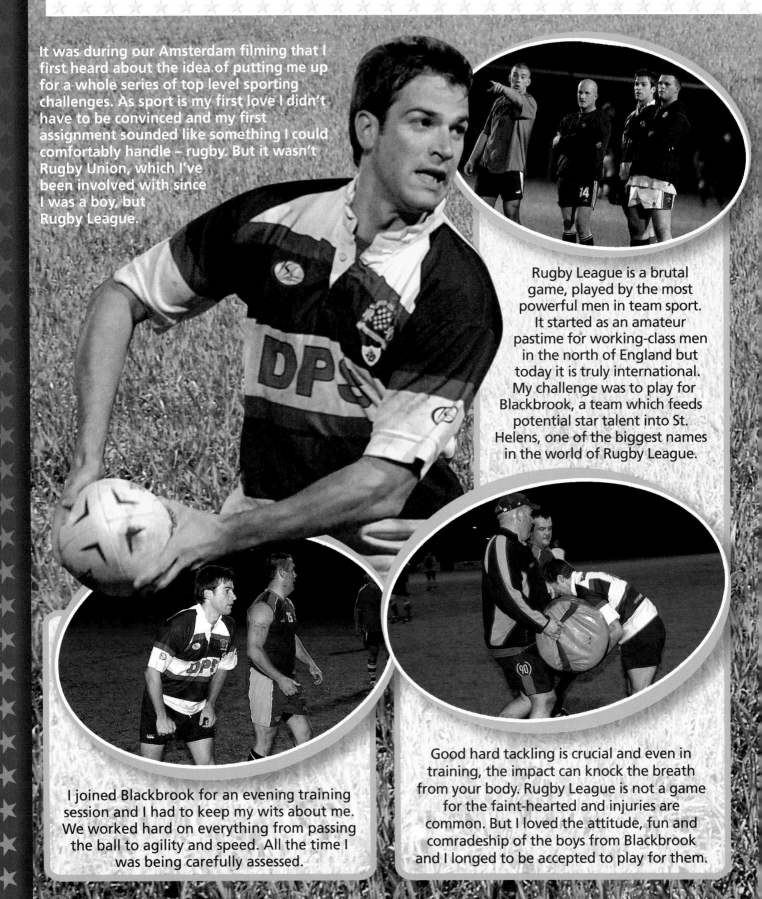

It was during our Amsterdam filming that I first heard about the idea of putting me up for a whole series of top level sporting challenges. As sport is my first love I didn't have to be convinced and my first assignment sounded like something I could comfortably handle – rugby. But it wasn't Rugby Union, which I've been involved with since I was a boy, but Rugby League.

Rugby League is a brutal game, played by the most powerful men in team sport. It started as an amateur pastime for working-class men in the north of England but today it is truly international. My challenge was to play for Blackbrook, a team which feeds potential star talent into St. Helens, one of the biggest names in the world of Rugby League.

I joined Blackbrook for an evening training session and I had to keep my wits about me. We worked hard on everything from passing the ball to agility and speed. All the time I was being carefully assessed.

Good hard tackling is crucial and even in training, the impact can knock the breath from your body. Rugby League is not a game for the faint-hearted and injuries are common. But I loved the attitude, fun and comradeship of the boys from Blackbrook and I longed to be accepted to play for them.

GO GETH

It seemed I'd done enough to impress them and a few days later, I joined the Blackbrook squad for a vital game in the first round of the Lancashire Cup. I wasn't here as a favour to some bloke off the telly. I was here to pull my weight.

I shoved in my gumshield and determined to do my best. Unknown to me, St Helens' star player Jon Wilkin, famous for carrying on playing with a broken nose and helping his team to their third Challenge Cup win in six years, was there to watch me and judge my efforts.

The match went by in a frenzy of speed and action. The result? We won 54-14 and the lads made a bit of a fuss of me. I was just delighted that I hadn't let them down and even more so when Jon told me I could pass for a professional. I was chuffed to bits. Have a Go Geth was off to a flying start.

Rugby League was far from easy but at least I was familiar with the game. The most experience I've had of high diving is watching it on tv. My challenge was to see whether I could go from a basic poolside dive to the head-spinning 7.5 metre board, all in one day. It was a tall order and I was scared from the start.

Perhaps that's why I made a mistake. The higher the dive, the more critical it is that your technique is perfect. I miscalculated and paid the price, smacking into the water and really hurting myself.

Olympic coach Adam Sotheran met me at the pool. He started by focusing on my not very advanced technique. Slowly he built up my confidence and I went from diving from the side of the pool to the one-metre board and from that to 3 metres and then on to 5 metres. I was still nervous but it certainly seemed to be going pretty well.

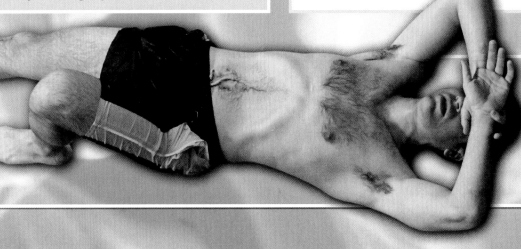

My back was in agony and little did I know but it was the start of an injury it would take weeks of treatment to recover from.

Straightaway, Adam got me stretching and at this point I still felt able to carry on. Having gone through so much, the last thing I wanted to do was walk away from the big one. The 7.5 metre dive. I made it to the top of the 7.5 metre board and looked down. You'll have heard people say "Don't look down" and it is good advice if you find heights a struggle. But I just had to see what I was letting myself in for and for a moment I felt completely sick. It seemed like an act of madness to even consider throwing myself off a diving board at that height.

the **Ultimate Swim**

Of course any dive is all over in a flash. But when I look at these photos, it brings back a few of the most super-charged seconds of my life. The dive was a total success.

P.S. Check out a couple more of my Have a Go Geth challenges on page 102.

No-one was forcing me to. It would be my decision. I felt more alone than I've ever done in my life before. Then I remembered something I'd been told when I was filming a gut-wrenching formation flying story for Blue Peter. "What the mind believes, the body achieves." The words echoed round my head and I knew it was now or never. I just hoped my freshly learnt technique wouldn't fail me again.

I emerged from the pool like a man possessed. I'd done it! Mind over matter had triumphed. Now I just had to sort out that throbbing pain in my back.

SOUPER CAKE

It is no mystery that I have a bit of a sweet tooth and I love this recipe for a yummy cake with an unusual secret ingredient. Condensed tomato soup. Sound a bit gross? I thought so too, until I tasted the end result. It really is easy to make, so give it a go and judge for yourself.

INGREDIENTS

THESE ARE THE INGREDIENTS YOU'LL NEED:

- 250g sugar
- 125g butter
- 2 eggs
- 1 tin of condensed tomato soup
- 180g raisins
- 1 teaspoon of bicarbonate of soda
- 120g plain flour
- 1 teaspoon baking powder
- 1 teaspoon mixed spice
- 100g walnut pieces (optional)
- Icing sugar to dust

STAGE 1

Put the butter and sugar into a large bowl. Using an electric whisk (a manual is fine but slightly harder work!), cream the butter and sugar together until they are light and fluffy.

Using a sieve, add the flour, baking powder and mixed spice and give it all a really good mix. Finally stir in the raisins and walnuts. If you or your family has a nut allergy, don't worry. It will taste just as good without them.

STAGE 2

Add the bicarbonate of soda, beat in the eggs and add your mystery ingredient – the condensed tomato soup. Mix all of these together.

STAGE 5

Take the cake out of the oven using oven gloves and leave to cool on a cooling rack. When it has cooled, lightly sprinkle some icing sugar over your cake and then it is time to test your friends and family to see if they can guess what your secret ingredient is!

STAGE 4

Pour the mixture into a cake tin. Preheat your oven to 180 degrees and put the cake in to to cook for about 45 minutes. A clever way to check that the cake is fully cooked through is to test it with a fork. If the fork comes out of the cake clean, with no sticky mixture on it, then it's ready!

Strictly Blue Peter

One of our favourite moments in the Blue Peter calendar is when we start to plan our Christmas entertainment. This year we decided to play our own tribute to the triumphant Saturday night success, *Strictly Come Dancing*. The only problem was that, unlike the stars of that show, we had precisely two days' rehearsal and one day in the studio to perfect four demanding and completely different dance routines.

Luckily, top choreographer and *Fame Academy* regular Kevin Adams was on hand to help. Kevin is well-known for being a hard taskmaster and his rehearsals are more boot camp than bright lights. He devised all the steps for the dances we'd decided to showcase – latin, disco, jive and the 1920s charleston.

There was no time to mess about. Zöe is the only one of us with any dance training and even she was finding it tough going. "Is the frown helping the dance?" barked Kevin. "I'm just concentrating," Zöe replied. "You should know it by now. Eyes and teeth. Smile!"

As the clock ticked away, we drilled each step relentlessly until at last they slowly began to come together. Kevin gave us some great advice. "Remember, even if you're not sure and you go wrong a bit – if you look totally confident and you really *perform* it, most people will never notice the mistakes."

We were recording our special in the BBC's biggest studio, Studio One at Television Centre. If you've ever wondered how the directors of *Strictly Come Dancing* get those wonderful, smooth-flowing, all-in-one shots of the action, the answer is by using one of these – a Steadicam. They're not cheap and they need expert camera operators to get the best out of them but the results are fabulous. With Steadicam, it's a bit like a dance in itself as the camera glides towards and around you.

Upstairs in the control gallery, Bridget, the director, watched our every move on a bank of monitors or tv screens. These show her the shots each of her five cameras were offering. It was Bridget's job to decide exactly which shots to use and when to cut to and from them. In its way, this is another kind of choreography and just as skilled as Kevin's. Bridget was also going to edit the whole day's recording into the finished ten-minute piece.

That job was going to be complicated because as well as playing the contestants, in Strictly Blue Peter, we were also playing the judges! Gethin had a tonne of orange make-up and sounded suspiciously like Craig Revel Horwood ("Three words. Must. Do. Better."), while Konnie was a dead ringer for Arlene Phillips ("You are what this competition is all about!"). Meanwhile, Andy and Zöe were both trying hard with their accents and the crew were trying hard not to laugh at them!

Strictly Blue Peter

As well as getting our dancing right, we had to look the part too. For the disco number, 'Can't Stop The Music', this meant groovy 1970s gear and an Afro wig for Andy. "I look like my brother," he pointed out as we hit the dance floor yet again. "He's a dude!"

We'd shared the vocals on the four tracks we were dancing to and it was weird hearing our own voices blaring out over the studio sound system. Professional dancers keep in time by counting the beats and bars which make up a song. But if you have to mime the words as well as count, it gets very complicated – a bit like simultaneously patting your head and rubbing your tummy.

We got through the disco and next it was another quick change into 1940s G.I. uniforms and dresses for the jive number 'Boogie Woogie Bugler Boy From Company B' – just try saying that out loud, never mind singing it at speed while you're dancing too! We knew we had to get this right before sweat patches started to spoil the look of the boys' uniforms. Gross but true!

By the time we moved on to the Charleston, we were all feeling the adrenaline that comes with performing under pressure. There was never a moment to spare and between Kevin giving us notes on the studio floor ("Smile! Look up and ahead! Don't look at your feet!") and Bridget giving us her notes from the gallery ("You're on camera two for shot 44 and don't creep too far downstage"), everyone was working their hardest to make the final take the best it could be.

We'd started rehearsing and recording at ten in the morning. Twelve hours later, everything was finally on tape and the Floor Manager told the studio that we had a clear. It was home-time! We were exhausted but happy. Even though we've all done a fair bit of dressing up and performing, Strictly Blue Peter had been a real challenge for us, as well being the most fantastic buzz. As Bruce and Tess say every Saturday night – "Keeeeep dancing!"

Countdown to Christmas

I just love the run-up to Christmas, finding presents for friends and families, enjoying parties and everything that goes with this special time of year. I'm a big fan of home-made decorations too, especially when they're as much fun as this fantastic Advent calendar. Why not have a go at making your own?

Materials

You'll need the following materials:

Coloured felt

White felt

Small pom-poms or cotton wool

Short lengths of wool or thread

Cord or ribbon

Rubber solution glue

Number stickers and some chocolates and small gifts to put inside the days

Stage 1

First of all, cut out stocking, mitten and Christmas party hat shapes as pictured. You could create your own template in paper first so the sizes match. Using different coloured felt, cut out four of each shape.

Stage 2

Glue around the edges and hold them together for a few seconds until the glue has dried. Alternatively, you could sew them together or use double-sided sticky tape.

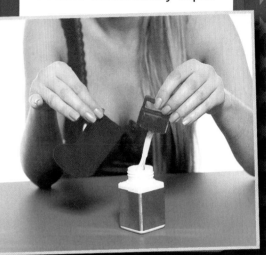

Stage 3

Cut some strips of white or different coloured felt and glue them on to create contrasting borders on your stockings, mittens and hats. Stick a pom-pom onto the end of the hat.

Stage 4

To add pom-poms to the stockings and mittens, tie a knot in the end of a piece of wool and using a needle, thread the other end through the pom-pom. Stick to the centre of the white felt strip and glue around the opening.

Stage 5

Get some number stickers from a craft shop. Stick the numbers 1 to 12 onto one side of each shape and then on the back glue the numbers 13 to 24 working backwards from 12 to 1. If you can't find stickers, you could just draw the numbers on circles of paper and stick these on instead.

Stage 6

To string all your stockings, mittens and hats together, thread some thin cord or ribbon through a needle. Push the needle through the side of each shape leaving about 10cm between each one. Tie a large loop at each end. You may need to stick a bit of tape either side of the shape to keep them in place.

Stage 7

To finish off, fill each shape, either with a chocolate treat or small gift. When you get to day 12, you can turn them around and re-fill the shapes for days 13-24. You could put in treats for your pets but remember that dogs mustn't eat the same chocolate we eat as it's not good for them. Hang your Advent calendar on a mantelpiece or wall.

Stage 8

To make the mobile version, you need a wire coat-hanger and some tinsel or shiny ribbon. First you need to flatten out the coat hanger. I'd suggest you get an adult to help you with this. Once it is in the right shape, wind the tinsel or ribbon around the hanger and secure the ends with sticky tape.

Then simply hang your finished shapes in four rows of three from the coat hanger and decide where you want to display your Advent calendar.

You could make one for yourself and give another as a present. Whichever version you decide to try, I think this is a decoration which makes that wonderful countdown to Christmas even more enjoyable!

Trooper Jones

I've done a little bit of riding on Blue Peter but I'm nowhere near the dazzling world class standard of the army's Household Cavalry regiment. They are the mounted soldiers who guard the Queen during all the most important state occasions.

My challenge is to reach the level where I can pass a riding inspection from the regiment's commanding officer. My instructor, Corporal of Horse 'Skip' Nicholls, was firm but fair. He even taught me the backwards dismount – an army speciality which is a bit like getting off a horse with a gymnastics move.

It wasn't just the riding I had to master. Eventually, I'd be in the saddle wearing the splendid full state uniform of a Trooper in the Household Cavalry. It weighs about three and half stone and fits very tight indeed. "We have a saying here Jones," they told me, "If it's comfortable, it doesn't fit."

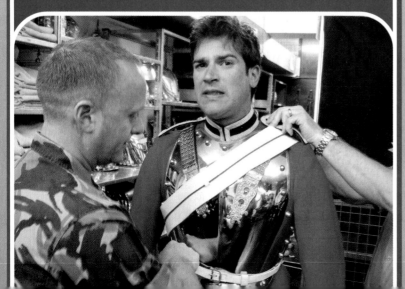

The boots make your legs feel as if they are in plaster and the chinstrap of the helmet makes it impossible to speak. Hot, hemmed in and weighed down, all the same I knew I looked the part. But could I convince the top brass that I was Trooper Jones of the Her Majesty's Life Guards and not Gethin Jones of Blue Peter? Keep watching to find out!

MAGIC MOMENTS

I'd hardly recovered from the excitement of getting the job on Blue Peter when I was told that I was going to be in charge of another new arrival – a golden retriever puppy, who at that point, had only just been born. The charity Guide Dogs For The Blind were celebrating their 75th birthday and it seemed just the right time for us to renew our friendship with them which goes back right to the very earliest days of the programme. Guide dogs make a massive difference to the life of a person with sight loss, offering them independence, freedom and confidence.

Guide Dogs' Breeding Manager Matthew Bottomley helped me pick out a female pup who seemed most suited to the twin challenge of becoming a guide dog and appearing regularly on television, with our cameras following every stage of her development. I'd had a puppy years before when I was still living in Nigeria and I knew that they are a huge responsibility, even when you're not attempting to prepare them for a life as a working dog. But let me tell you, it was love at first sight!

The plan was for me to take on the important job of training of a guide dog puppy so just a few days after I'd got my badge, it was off to Warwickshire to meet Willow, the proud mother of a litter of four beautiful eight-week old pups.

Guide dogs are all given names beginning with a letter which tells you what year they were born – a bit like car registrations. It rotates through the alphabet and 2006's letter was M. We asked Blue Peter viewers to come up with a name beginning with M and we were inundated with 43,825 suggestions – over 10,000 of them within an hour of Matthew selecting our pup from the litter live on air. Top favourites included Molly, Maestro, Muffin and Marbles. On October 16th, there was a drumroll and you could hear a pin drop in the studio as we revealed the chosen name – Magic!

Taking Magic out and about was an important part of her training. Matthew came with us on this particular trip, when Magic was twelve weeks old. It was designed to take in lots of the sights, sounds and smells you find in the heart of a busy city like London. Matthew explained that it is very easy for a young puppy to get distracted or frightened and so this walk would be a real test for her. She did well with the traffic, even staying calm when several impatient motorists started tooting their horns in the queue.

But when we reached Trafalgar Square, I noticed that Magic was tugging at her lead a lot more than usual. Guide dogs need excellent concentration to help their owners so I was worried that this might be where the outing proved too much of a challenge for her.

To be fair, the reason for Magic's distraction was perfectly understandable. Trafalgar Square is famous for its hordes of pigeons and even though the Mayor of London has attempted to have the numbers controlled, the pigeons keep getting the better of him. As they fluttered about, cooing away, completely unflustered by pedestrians or small dogs, Magic was wagging her tail and bounding ahead, obviously dead keen to investigate.

I tried her with the command to sit – and it worked. Then on we went. Magic was doing well with the basic commands I'd been taught to use with her but of course there's a big difference between the controlled, reliable surroundings of our studio and the chaos of central London. Matthew told me not to worry about the occasional lapses of control and command. All in all, he felt that she was doing very well. "And you're not doing so bad yourself," he added.

MAGIC MOMENTS

By now, Magic was used to travelling by car but she'd never been on the water before so I was interested to see how she'd react to taking a ride on a water taxi down the River Thames. She was as good as gold, sniffing the salty air and taking it all in her stride. As she sat on my lap and we chugged through the choppy water, I could easily sense the strong bond which builds up between a guide dog and its owner.

We reached our destination in Westminster. So far Magic had done well with different kinds of traffic and people. Now Matthew suggested it might be a good idea to see how she would react to a larger animal. The local Metropolitan mounted police had agreed to let us pay a visit to their stables. As soon as we arrived, Magic was fascinated by these strange and towering new creatures. Police horses are trained every bit as well as guide dogs so there was no danger but Magic could have reacted very differently. Happily, she showed no fear at all.

At the end of the afternoon, there was one last test in store, a trip on the London Eye and reunion with her brothers and sisters, all of them now in training to become guide dogs themselves. Magic wasn't a bit bothered about getting inside the pod or the sensation of it moving up higher and higher. She just seemed delighted to see the rest of her litter again. Trying to take this photograph took a lot of effort as all the pups had one thing on their minds – play!

The studio soon became a second home for Magic. In a way, being surrounded by the crew and all the technical equipment was another training hurdle for her to overcome. The biggest problem was persuading the other presenters, the production team and any visitors that I couldn't allow Magic to play all the time or accept treats or snacks between her official meal times. It sounds strict but if I was too relaxed at this stage, it might mean she'd fail her tests in weeks to come. Luckily, everyone was very understanding.

The other bonus was that the Blue Peter garden is close by and this meant we could always nip out of the studio whenever we had a break for a bit of a romp and a brush up on any part of her training which I felt needed extra attention. I tried always to be patient with Magic and remember that we had to go at her pace. In return, I think she was pretty patient with me too!

Over the months, we've shared all her ups and downs. It hasn't always been plain sailing. She has had her setbacks and a few bouts of illness. But overall, Magic has a nature to match her name. Helping to puppy-walk her has been a highlight of my first year on the programme and when the moment comes for her to move on to her advanced training, I'll be both over the moon at her success and sad to say goodbye. Of course there is a small risk she won't pass the advanced stage – just over a quarter of selected pups don't make it and have to be found ordinary homes. If she is one of the successful ones, it is wonderful to think that she will transform the life of her eventual owner. Magic has already had a big impact on mine and, whatever happens, I know we'll be keeping in touch.

AULD REEKIE

Auld Reekie is a Scots nickname for Edinburgh and it dates back to the days when the chimneys here constantly spewed filthy smoke from coal and wood fires, making the city smell pretty bad. Happily these days Auld Reekie is just a nickname, and as I stood on the walls of Edinburgh Castle I got a magnificent view of Scotland's beautiful capital city.

I'd come here for a special Burns Night Blue Peter. Burns Night takes place every January 25th and it is named after Scotland's most famous poet, Robert or Rabbie Burns. For Scottish people all over the world, it's basically an excuse for a big party with traditional food like haggis (spicy meat in a sheep's stomach – delicious!), neeps (turnips) and tatties (potatoes) and a big celilidh or highland dance.

For many Scotsmen, Burns Night parties mean wearing the kilt. There's an old saying which goes "a man in a kilt is a man and a half" and I certainly felt good in mine. But these days classic Highland wear is usually seen only on formal occasions like weddings and parties. One man would like to change that. He's Howie Nicholsby who runs 21st Century Kilts. As the name suggests, Howie creates kilts for the modern man, in all kinds of styles and fabrics. He suggested I should try out some of his favourite designs.

This kilt is made from camouflage material. I thought it looked great teamed with some chunky boots and thick socks. I got quite a few compliments from passers-by too!

I'd never heard of a kilt suit before but this brown pinstripe was very smart. Don't ask me what I was doing though – it was the photographer's idea!

One thing about the kilt you notice straightaway – it is really comfortable to wear.

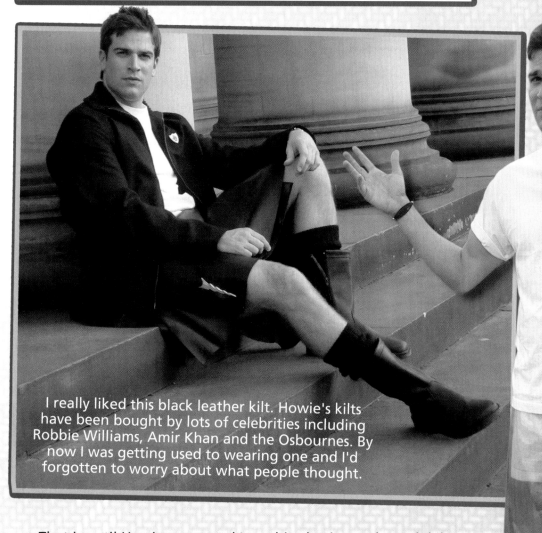

I really liked this black leather kilt. Howie's kilts have been bought by lots of celebrities including Robbie Williams, Amir Khan and the Osbournes. By now I was getting used to wearing one and I'd forgotten to worry about what people thought.

That is until Howie suggested I try this plastic see-through kilt. I walked along Edinburgh's Princes Street during rush hour, expecting people to point, laugh and comment – but most of them didn't bat an eyelid. I was just grateful I was wearing clean underwear!

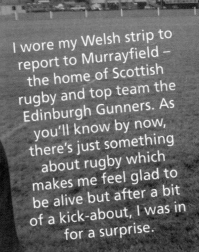

I wore my Welsh strip to report to Murrayfield – the home of Scottish rugby and top team the Edinburgh Gunners. As you'll know by now, there's just something about rugby which makes me feel glad to be alive but after a bit of a kick-about, I was in for a surprise.

Scottish rugby star and Gunner Chris Paterson suggested I try out the players' bath. But this was no ordinary bath – it was full of icy water. The players go in for three-minute bursts after training because the freezing cold is good for their muscles and circulation. Chris told me to jog on the spot. When I asked why, he grinned and explained that it stops the body forming any insulation around itself. In other words, the cold has more impact. Lovely!

The most common question about the kilt is what does a Scotsman wear underneath? The answer is supposed to be nothing. But as I come from Cardiff, I played safe and wore some Welsh rugby shorts.

Just when I thought it couldn't get any worse, Chris decided the water needed topping up and poured a bucket of fresh ice all over me. I muttered something under my breath. "Speak up, Geth," he suggested, smiling happily but I was shivering too much to say any more.

These guys don't mind a bit of cold water. They're the penguins of Edinburgh Zoo, a top attraction free to Blue Peter badge-winners. Every day, the keepers carefully place extra vitamin tablets inside the fish to keep the penguins in peak condition. It was fantastic to get so close to them – even when one of them took a peck at my legs. Kilts do have some disadvantages!

Nevertheless, it was back into another one when I reported to the Army School of Bagpipe Music and Highland Drumming. Bagpipes are the sound of Scotland. Over the years, many Blue Peter presenters have had a go at playing them but the pipes are notoriously difficult to master. Could I be the first presenter to get a tune out of them?

My instructor said his name was Martin but the lesson was so strict and formal I kept wanting to call him Sir and put my hand up whenever I wanted to ask anything.

I joined a classroom of pipers in training. The first stage is to learn to play the chanter, the bit of the bagpipes which actually makes the tune.

Luckily, Martin took pity on me and suggested I'd benefit from some one-to-one instruction. He told me it was time to add the chanter to the bags – and start my attempts at playing the bagpipes for real. I couldn't believe the effort it takes to keep the bags filled with air and concentrate on the fingerwork at the same time.
Spit was going everywhere and my face changed colour a few times but I was determined not to be beaten.

Out of one uniform and into another. The pupils of the Mary Erskine and Stewart's Melville Junior School had invited me to join in their Burns Night celebrations. I thought I'd surprise them by turning up in their distinctive school uniform!

The end of my training came at last and I was really nervous as Martin gave me the command to begin playing Robert Burns' classic 'Scots, Wha Hae'. Two military drummers began to beat out the rhythm. I expanded my chest as far as I could and to my amazement, out came the tune – deafeningly loud but very nearly perfect. At the end of my recitation, I was given a spontaneous round of applause. Martin smiled, satisfied at a job well done. "You're nae bad," he told me. "A few months' work and we could make a piper of you."

The school has a great reputation for drama and had agreed to help us recreate a glimpse of what life was like in the bad old days when Edinburgh's schools were some of the toughest in Scotland. I was playing two parts – one of the scary schoolmaster....

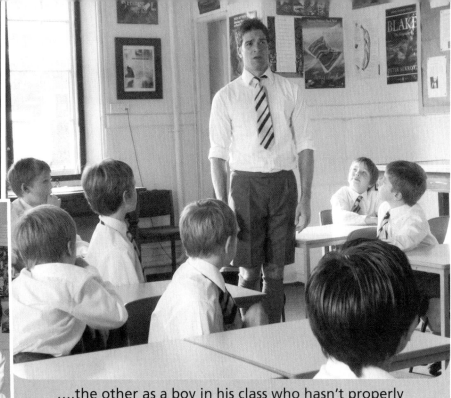

....the other as a boy in his class who hasn't properly learnt his homework, a Rabbie Burns poem.

Right up until the 1980s, Scottish teachers used a tawse, or belt as it was known, to punish children, hitting them on the palms of their upturned hands. It was very painful and I should know because during the filming, to make sure it looked realistic, I was hit several times!

We used television trickery to achieve the effect of me punishing myself. On location in the school, I had to play the scene twice, in each different costume. Then back in the Blue Peter editing suite, the two halves of the shot were put together. It looked very effective but all the boys who helped with the filming agreed that it was a good thing the tawse is now part of Edinburgh's past.

I wore my 21st century kilt on our Christmas show and it brought back memories of the very happy week I'd spent filming in Edinburgh.

Konnie Huq

In my ten years on Blue Peter, I've presented nearly 1000 programmes and had so many adventures I lose count. I've sung, danced, acted, travelled all over the world, interviewed everyone from Prince William to the Prime Minister, presented countless cooks and makes and awarded hundreds of badges. But until we launched our Bash Street Kid competition, I'd never been turned into a comic strip character.

It wasn't a very dignified experience. And I'm sure my nose isn't really that big. But maybe that's being hyper sensitive. After all, I suppose you shouldn't expect good manners from the Bash Street Kids. They've been the rowdy stars of *The Beano* for over fifty years now. *The Beano* itself has been going since 1938 and it is still one of Britain's most successful comics.

Together with our friends at DC Thomson, who produce *The Beano*, we were offering a unique prize for the winner of our competition. The chance to create a brand new Bash Street character to join the gang on a permanent basis. I wasn't surprised that we had 26,349 entries and you can see the winning design on page 109, as well as, of course, in the pages of *The Beano* itself. Their artists have also had a go at cartoon versions of Zöe, Gethin and Andy too – check their profile pages for the results.

Meanwhile, back to my own comic strip mini-masterpiece and Cartoon Konnie made a quick getaway. With that reception, I don't blame her!

COLD COMFORTS

Don't ask me how Gethin and I managed to end up standing by a freezing cold outdoor swimming pool at the beginning of January. I think it was our Editor's idea of a joke. "It's the latest thing!" he told us, "Hydrotherapy and kriotherapy. You'll love it! Kind of spa treatments. New Year, new you." Then, before we could get a word in edgeways, he reminded me that I'd Try Anything Once and that Geth was now known as Have a Go Geth. We decided we'd better just get on with it.

"Can this really be happening?" I asked myself. I was looking to Geth for some support but he *is* a boy, I suppose, and what do all boys love doing at the pool? Pushing. He gave me an almighty shove to get me in and followed with a great splash of his own. At least the suspense was over with.

So here we were, first thing in the morning, teeth chattering with the cold, trying to get up the courage to jump in at the deep end of the Tooting Lido pool. We were told that regular swimmers here swear by a regular cold plunge in the depth of winter. They reckon it is the best way to ward off colds and flu.

I think our expressions say it all. It was brutally cold in there and for a moment I think I even forgot how to swim. "Come on, Salmon, kick your legs, it'll warm you up," said Geth. "How rude," I managed to mutter in the middle of a violent shiver.

The blue towels we were handed when we'd completed our swim were almost the same colour as we were. But, although I would never have admitted it at the time, I was quickly aware of a pleasant glowing feeling all over my body. In fact, the use of cold water to sooth pains and treat illnesses is hundreds of years old. It's called hydrotherapy.

Rich Victorians went to spas and clinics to try all the latest techniques. One involved drinking countless glasses of cold water to cleanse the body. Which basically means you have to wee a lot. All very well but you try clambering out of a crinoline and several layers of underwear in a hurry.

This was the era of the 'stiff upper lip' and men often pretended to be fond of a bracing dip in the local pond or river. Children didn't have it any easier. They frequently had to start the day with a cold bath or shower to toughen them up as well as get them clean.

The Victorians certainly didn't do hydrotherapy by halves. This is the 'descending douche', said to be "most refreshing". It reminded Gethin of his ice bath in the Edinburgh Gunners players' pool. "Don't know what I was complaining about really," he told me, as another couple of buckets hit us from above.

COLD COMFORTS

Damp, bedraggled and frozen though we were, it wasn't the end of the treatment. Now we were wrapped in ice-cold sheets and were told to lie down and relax in them for a few minutes. The Victorians swore by this method for treating inflammations, fevers and conditions like arthritis and rheumatism. Perhaps the theory was – numb yourself with cold and feel no pain? Or indeed anything at all?

At least it was indoors and back to modern methods for our next treatment. Kriotherapy is the latest health craze and trying it out involved wearing outfits I thought would be more at home in an exercise class. But by this point, I just decided to do what I was told.

These masks stop your breath from freezing in the extreme temperature of minus 130 degrees you encounter when you enter the Kriotherapy chamber.

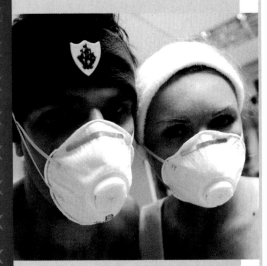

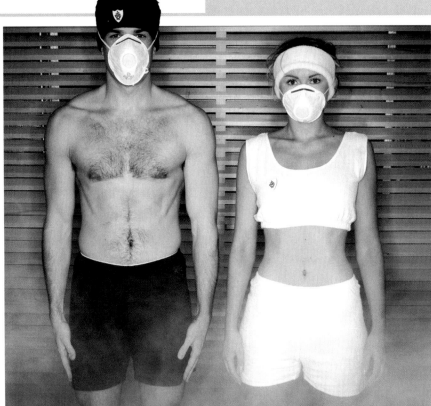

Imagine stepping inside a giant deep-freeze. That's what it felt like to me. You're supposed to have several three-minute sessions to reap the maximum benefit. The theory behind its benefits are more or less the same as those of swimming in cold water.

The fierce cold forces your system to withdraw blood to the body's core to maintain its temperature. Once the treatment is over the same blood is pumped vigorously back around the body, boosting your immune system by encouraging the body to produce more of the cells which attack bugs and viruses.

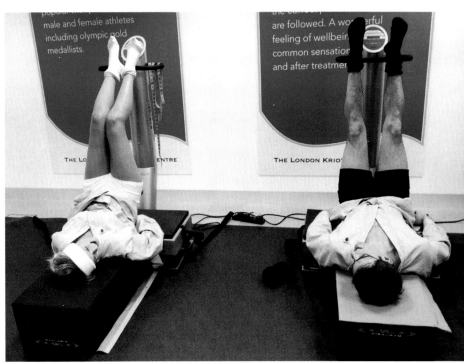

After the process, it was off to do some warm-up exercises – which seemed odd to me as you usually do your warm-up before you exercise and not after! This weird contraption was the vibro gym. You lie back and try to relax while a series of plates manipulate your lower back and the vibration helps promote the flow of blood round your body. Geth found it really helpful for the back pain he'd picked up doing his high dive.

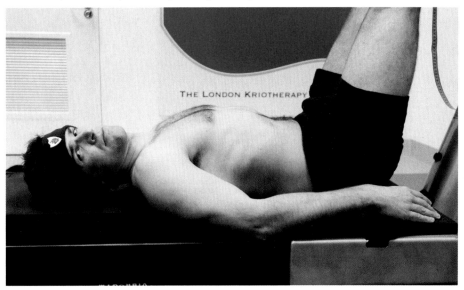

Finally, we were left to relax. What a day! We certainly both felt invigorated but could that just have been because the ordeal was over? "Never again!," I said to Geth. And I meant it too. At that moment, my mobile rang. It was our Editor again. "How did it go?," he asked me. I took a sip of the delicious orange juice I'd been given. "Oh you know me – I'll Try Anything Once..." Geth beside me spoke up, "And I'm Have a Go Geth!".

I suppose we're really our own worst enemies...

The Voyage Of Jemmy Button

Today Walthamstow is a busy part of East London. Two hundred years ago, a young boy arrived here after travelling thousands of miles from his home in Tierra del Fuego, just off the coast of South America. I went in search of his incredible story.

1 This was the time when British adventurers were exploring the world and the Commander of *HMS Beagle*, Robert Fitzroy, was fascinated by the idea of what might happen if he took some of the Fuegian Indians back home with him. The Fuegians loved anything bright and shining and so it was that Fitzroy persuaded a boy called Orundellico to join his ship in exchange for a button. In honour of the deal, Orundellico was given a new European name, Jemmy Button.

2 Jemmy was given sailors' clothes and plenty of fresh food to keep him well on the long journey. Fitzroy wrote: "Jemmy joined three other Fuegians on board our ship. All were in high spirits. My hope is that they will learn something of our world before I keep my promise to return them home."

3 As the long voyage took them ever closer to Britain, *HMS Beagle* was passed by a brand new steam ship. With its enormous funnel belching steam and its speed and noise, it was the very latest in ship design. But to Jemmy it was more like a roaring sea monster and when he saw it, he cowered in fear.

4 At last they arrived in Britain and in December 1830, Jemmy and his friends set off for London the fastest way possible by stage-coach. Jemmy was especially impressed by the repeated changes of horses used to speed up the journey to Walthamstow.

5 The name Walthamstow actually means "place where guests are welcome" and the people of Walthamstow made a great fuss of the Fuegians. Jemmy loved his new clothes and stepped out smartly to services at St Mary's Church in his best suit, gloves and gleaming boots. His charm and spirit made him a great favourite with all who met him.

6 Jemmy attended lessons in the local school and proved he had a sharp mind and a quick sense of humour. It helped that each lesson was only 15 minutes long as there was no time to get bored!

7 As very few people travelled in those days, the Fuegian visitors quickly became the talk of London. His Majesty King William IV and Queen Adelaide invited them to St James' Palace where the King asked a great many questions and the Queen gave them gifts.

8 The visit had been a great success but Commander Fitzroy was determined to keep his promise to take Jemmy and his friends back home to Tierra del Fuego. The first stage of the epic return trip was by the steam vessel *Shannon*. Thirteen months earlier Jemmy had been scared out of his wits by a ship just like this one. Now he didn't bat an eyelid.

9 Once he was back on board *HMS Beagle* again, Jemmy made friends with a man called Charles Darwin. Jemmy kept him company when Darwin was seasick, muttering "poor, poor fellow!". Darwin was working on his famous book *Origin of the Species*, which argued that humans had not been created by God but had evolved like all living things, gradually, over time.

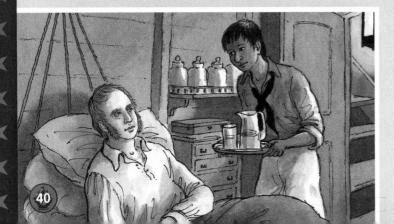

10 Darwin was fascinated by Jemmy's ability to spot ships or dangerous rocks far out to sea, long before anyone else. His theory was that the Fuegians' eyesight had evolved to become so powerful simply because it was essential to their survival. Darwin's theories were revolutionary, changing the way people thought about the creation and development of life. They are still argued about today.

11 Jemmy arrived back in Tierra del Fuego in February 1833. But sadly his homecoming was a disaster. The Europeans had brought new diseases with them and the Fuegians had no resistance to them. Jemmy eventually fell victim to one of these infections and died. Within a few decades, the Fuegian Indians had been wiped out altogether.

12 When I visited Walthamstow, I found some parts of the area which Jemmy would still recognise, like the school he went to and St Mary's Church, where he attended services dressed in his finest clothes. Although Jemmy's story has a sad end, his life wasn't wasted. His friendship with Charles Darwin helped shape some of the most important new ideas the world has ever seen. Just as importantly, he's remembered for his courage, intelligence and good humour, all of which carried him through his incredible voyage.

DUE SOUTH

Here we are in front of what became our base for our Summer Expedition to the Southern States of the USA. It's a giant motor-home and we slept here, ate here and tried not to get on each other's nerves too much as we covered thousands of miles in our mission to go deep into a huge area of America that Blue Peter has never explored in-depth before.

Looking back, the jump itself is all a bit of a blur. I remember the count – 5,4,3,2,1 – and the next thing I knew, I was flying through the air with the wind rushing past my ears. It was an unbelievably exhilarating feeling and the stomach-scrambling sensation of such an extreme jump was quickly followed by elation and pride that I'd actually conquered my fear and taken that leap of faith at all.

It was my first summer trip and it started with the biggest challenge of my life so far – I was going to get a bird's eye view of the Southern States by taking a bungee jump from a helicopter thousands of metres up. The only thing I'm really afraid of is heights and I spent ages wondering if I could really put myself through this. Put it this way, I'd skipped breakfast before my meeting with the expert heli-bungee team who were in charge. But before I knew it, I was harnessed up and ready to bungee and there was just time to kiss the rope on which my life would depend.

If you like cars which make a statement, check out this baby. Geth and I were taking a detour from life on the road to try out life on the ranch in Texas. There are many thousands of cattle in the Southern States all helping to feed the American appetite for steak and burgers.

Neither of us has much experience on the back of a horse but we'd both seen plenty of cowboy movies and we both tried to seem as if we knew one side of a saddle from another.

But we weren't just there to look the part. A few quick lessons from a real-life cowboy and I was trying my hardest to lasso one of the cattle and stay on my horse at the same time. I was quite pleased with my efforts but I don't think the herd were in any doubt that I was an amateur.

All over the South, you can find great plantations or farms with a big house. For their white owners, it was a graceful world of carriages and balls. But the money to support this grand lifestyle came from slavery. It took a civil war to end slavery but black people stayed far worse off than white. Sadly there is still a lot of racism and discrimination in the South.

NASA MISSION CONTROL CENTER

The techniques used to train space crews are incredibly advanced. This is me at the controls of a space shuttle simulator which goes far beyond anything you'll find in a theme park. I was actually allowed to 'land' the shuttle and I amazed Zöe by not crashing! It was such an adrenaline rush.

For me, the highlight of the trip came when Zöe and I were given VIP access to NASA in Houston – the centre of all the world's top space missions and astronaut training.

Climbing inside a real space suit is a claustrophobic experience but not as hot as you might think thanks to the highly sophisticated built-in cooling system. Inside the helmet, there's even a tiny attachment so an astronaut can deal with an itchy nose!

Meanwhile, as Geth and Zöe were staring into space, I was getting ready to dive deep beneath the ocean. I'd been given the chance to join a team investigating the wreck of an old cargo ship. There used to be plenty of pirates in this area but sadly I didn't find any pirate gold.

Lloyd and his 12-year-old son ZZ have a very unusual job. They capture stray alligators and return them safely to the wild. I think my expression says it all – never in my wildest dreams did I imagine I'd end up sitting on a highly dangerous alligator's back. As the saying goes, it's a tough job – but someone's got to do it!

Every August, thousands of people converge on Gracelands in Memphis, Tennessee, now a museum but once the home of legendary Mississippi-born singer Elvis Presley. They flock here to take part in a massive candle-lit vigil to commemorate his death. We all found it strangely moving.

Our expedition took place almost exactly a year after the devastating Hurricane Katrina and, as we discovered in Louisiana's New Orleans, much of the damage was still being cleared up. Crumpled houses and wrecked streets were everywhere we looked. Although America is a rich nation, many of the worst affected people were its poorest citizens and that's the sad reason why the clean-up has taken so long.

Even though he died way back in 1977, Elvis or 'the King' as his fans call him, is still big business and much of his music has a real flavour of the Southern States about it. We finished off our trip with our own tribute to the King, a version of his number one hit, 'A Little Less Conversation'. It was a suitable title too as our Elvis impressions left quite a few of the crowds who watched us film it lost for words.

Dolls' DINER

DINER

During our summer expedition to the Southern States of the USA, we all enjoyed eating in classic American diners just like this one. It gave me the idea for this authentic miniature version, perfect if your dolls and action figures enjoy chilling out by the jukebox, with a shake, burger and fries...

DINER

ICE CREAM

AMERICAN DAIRY Co. ICE CREAM

Menu
Dolls' Diner

Stage One

First you'll need a large cardboard box. Cut away the top and front of the box and the front half of one side, leaving about 20cm. Paint the walls a neutral colour like cream and the floor black. Cover the card with a large check design in sticky-backed plastic or alternatively, you can paint the design yourself. Place the finished floor inside the box.

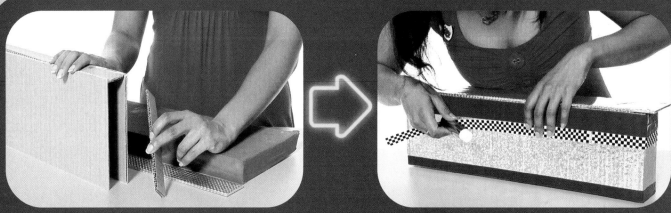

Stage Two

For the counter, cut a piece of card 7cm shorter than the width of your box and 7cm wide. This will be the top of your counter. Two pieces of card 49 by 13.5cm will form the front and back. Tape these together and cover the sides with silver holographic paper. Stick two rows of red tape around the top and one small row of small checks underneath. Cut another piece of card 2cm wider than your counter top and cover this with the same silver paper before sticking it on top of the counter.

Stage Three

To make the back shelf, cut a 3cm wide strip of card to fit along the back wall and two pieces 17cm long. Tape the short pieces to each end of the long one. Then cut two pieces of card the width of the long strip by 17cm high. Tape these to each side of the strip. Paint your shelf unit dark grey and once it has dried, cut a piece of card to fit the top and cover with silver holographic paper before sticking to the top of the shelf.

Stage Four

Make the stools by cutting a circle of wadding and sticking it on a drinks bottle lid. Cut a circle of red leatherette fabric and place over the wadding. Snip the outer edge of this and tape to the lid with sticky tape, pulling the fabric as you go. Stick some silver paper around the side of the lid. Next cut a piece of silver card 11.5 by 8cm. Draw a line 1.5cms from the edge along the short side and snip at intervals up to the line. Use a pen to help roll the card into a tube. Tape to secure. Bend and spread out the tabs.

Stage Five

Cut a circle of thin card to fit inside the lid. Spread some all-purpose glue inside the lid and push the card circle inside. Spread the other side of the circle with glue and stick to the silver tabs of the tube. To reinforce the seat, cut a circle of thick card with a small hole in the centre for the tube to fit through. Push this up to the lid until it is a snug fit. The base is a rubber tea towel holder painted silver. Just push the end of the tube into the holder.

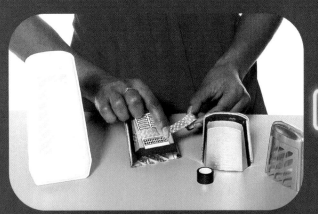

Stage Six

To make the jukebox, cut the top 7cm from an air freshener, paint silver and leave to dry. Cover the back with red holographic paper and add a strip of red around the front. Draw the record selection controls onto a piece of paper and stick to the front of the jukebox. Finish with a strip of silver paper across the front and place your jukebox on the counter against the side wall.

Stage Seven

Use the inside box of a large matchbox and individual cereal packets as the basis of your cabinets. Use the left-over bits to make shelves by cutting a strip to fit the width of your box. Paint the cabinets silver. A small clear plastic box with a door cut from clear plastic and the inside painted dark grey makes another type of cabinet.

Stage Eight

For the bench seat units, first you need a base, cut from a 10 by 10cm piece of cardboard. Tape 2cm wide strips round each side and then tape the corners together to form a base. Paint or cover with sticky-backed plastic.

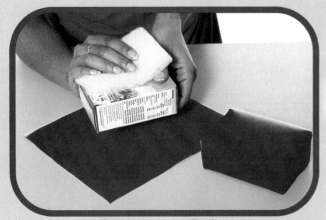

Stage Nine

To make the seats, cut a piece of wadding the same size as one of the large sides of an individual cereal packet and stick it on. Cut a piece of red leatherette 22 by 20cm and place over the wadding. Cut away at the corners and pull the fabric around the box and tape underneath.

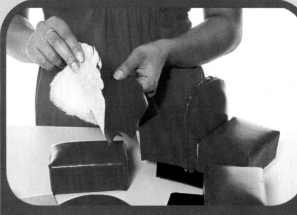

Stage Ten

Cut two pieces of cardboard to make the backs and stick on a piece of wadding. Then cover as before with red leatherette before sticking the two backs together. You assemble your seat unit by sticking one seat either side of the back piece and then fixing it to the base. To make a single seat, simply make your base half as wide and only use one cereal packet.

Stage Eleven

Next the tables. Cut your table top from a foil food container. If you add a 1cm border, you can bend this round a piece of cardboard to strengthen your table top. Then cut 11.5cm from a small cardboard tube and cover with silver paper 2cm longer to overhang at the end. Snip this overhang at intervals and bend the flaps back. Stick to the table top. For the base, cut a circle of silver card 5.5cm in width. Draw around the tube in the centre and cut slits from the centre to the drawn line and bend the flaps out. Spread glue round the end of the tube and stick the flaps to the tube. Cover any jagged edges with silver paper.

Stage Twelve

For the all-important finishing touches, make plates cut from the base of small yoghurt drinks bottles. 1cm pieces of wooden dowel painted white look like mugs. If you paint one end brown, it will look as if it is full of coffee. You could photocopy the menus on page 46 and stick them onto card. Posters and signs can be downloaded from the internet. Finally, why not try making tiny burgers and sundaes from modelling clay? Then you're all ready to start serving your customers!

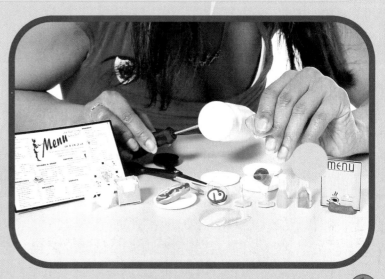

SOCKS AT THE SHOW

The annual National Cat Club Championship at the Olympia Exhibition Centre in Birmingham is the biggest cat show in Britain and as well as the long list of classes for all the different breeds, it is also home to the Blue Peter best-in-show non-pedigree category.

With so many cats at the show, it's a strict regulation that every single one of them has to be seen by a vet before they go on show. The vet took a close look at Socks' ears, eyes, teeth and skin and I was delighted that he passed his check-up with flying colours.

Andy and I were invited to help judge the category and to bring Socks along as guest of honour. I decided to try him on his new lead and I was very impressed that Socks didn't seem to bat an eyelid, despite the crowds and the fact that there were around 550 other cats on the premises. His laid-back personality is one of the reasons we all love him.

As well as a chance for Socks to meet his fans, we had our own Blue Peter stand where we chatted with viewers and signed autographs. Many of them had travelled a long way to show their cats.

Andy and I posed for pictures with Socks before we set off to do our bit as judges of the Blue Peter classes.

As ever, it was really difficult to make the selection of the top three cats who'd battle it out in the studio for the coveted title of Blue Peter's Cat of the Year. But in the end, we made our decision and the final three were Freddy with owner 14-year-old Theresa Kennedy, Mascara with 11-year-old Joseph Allwright and Alfie with 12-year-old Hannah Hardman.

There was a drumroll as we announced the winner – Freddy, who is a beautiful blue silver semi-longhaired tabby. Theresa told us that Freddy is the purr-fect pet who likes to stow himself away in the car so that he can join in family trips and outings! Like all our previous winners, Theresa and Freddy won a special rosette and the Blue Peter silver cup trophy, which is theirs to keep forever. Well done to both of them!

Stars In Their Eyes

Ever wondered what it's like to star on stage or screen? When I was growing up, I certainly did and eventually I auditioned for and was accepted by the National Youth Music Theatre. It was a great experience and other members from my time included film star Jude Law and comedy actor Matt Lucas. I even appeared on Blue Peter, aged 17 – and won my first badge into the bargain. The NYMT was my first step towards working in television.

It may be hard work but I could see why he loves it. There is something magical about the theatre, with its distinctive smell of dust, paint and electricity. Piers told me that there are strict rules controlling how long children can work so *The Sound of Music* has three complete sets of children to share the eight shows a week.

Backstage at the world-famous London Palladium, I met 12-year-old Piers Stubbs, who plays Kurt in the smash-hit musical *The Sound of Music*. Piers goes to a theatre school and one of the first things he learnt there was just how strong the competition can be. Before he got the part, he had to audition alongside hundreds of others. Now he's actually appearing in the show, he has to sing, dance and act his heart out four times a week while keeping up a full diary of lessons and homework.

Audiences pay top prices for seats in London's West End so they expect the very best singing. Before every performance, Piers and his fellow cast members go through a careful vocal warm-up to get their voices ready. I joined them for a session and I was amazed at the focus and sheer dedication of the young cast. Piers sang his solo lines from the Lonely Goatherd song and I thought they sounded great. But the vocal coach had other ideas. "Crisper, clearer, again!" she rapped out. Piers didn't seem to mind. It was all part of the job.

After I'd had the chance to look around the theatre, I invited Piers and his co-stars to perform The Lonely Goatherd in the Blue Peter studio. The leading part of Maria is played by Connie Fisher, who won the role as part of the BBC talent search *How Do You Solve a Problem Like Maria?* She'd never met another Connie – even though I spell mine with a K!

There are lots of costume changes in *The Sound of Music* and for speed, buttons and zips are often replaced with Velcro. Piers said you can't worry about looking silly. The clothes may be the last thing most boys would choose to wear but they are exactly right for the character and story, which is set in the 1930s. This meant a short back and sides too. Before he joined the show, Piers had long hair but that would have been all wrong for a member of the Von Trapp family.

To make them feel at home, we all dressed up in traditional Austrian outfits too. Geth was a bit put out at how funny they thought he looked!

We had to rehearse the number several times for lighting and cameras and I was impressed at how the young actors were able to deliver the same precision with every line and movement time after time. Making it all look effortless is the sign of a real professional. I asked Piers if he ever got nervous. "Sometimes," he admitted, "But when the performance starts, the excitement of that takes over."

Perhaps not surprisingly, Piers would like to keep acting when he grows up. If he does stick at it, we think that Piers Stubbs will be a name to watch out for in years to come. But Piers wasn't the only potential star of the future to feature on Blue Peter this year.

We launched one of our most exciting competitions ever surrounded by monsters! The once-in-a-lifetime prize was to win a speaking part in an episode of *Dr Who*. The *Dr Who* scripting team wrote three different audition pieces and in total, 8113 viewers took the trouble to choose one of them, learn their lines and send in their tapes, some from as far way as Australia.

We eventually narrowed our selection down to a top ten, who were all invited to spend the day at a special acting workshop at London's Globe Theatre. Joanne, Vigo, Stephanie, John, Sophie, Jennifer, Aidan, Jonathan, Lizzie and Billy had done brilliantly well to get through and although spirits were high, they knew that there was only one part on offer.

The judges were Blue Peter's Editor Richard Marson, actress Annette Badland, who played one of the Doctor's monstrous enemies, the Slitheen, and *Dr Who's* casting director Andy Pryor. It is Andy's job to cast all the main parts in *Dr Who* and he had high expectations: "Whoever gets the part will be on set filming with professional actors on a very busy shoot. They have to be up to the challenge."

Stars In Their Eyes

Soon after they'd arrived, the ten were divided into pairs and each pair spent several hours working on a specially written *Dr Who* scene. Just before lunch, each pair acted out their scene in front of the judges. There was no doubt about it. There was a lot of talent in the room and it was going to be hard to choose.

But somehow the judges had to reduce the ten down to a final three. It really was agonising, not just because the standard was so high but because by now, everyone had bonded and it felt so painful to send anybody home. At long last, the decision was made. The news was broken to the group and by the end, there were quite a few tears.

John

Lizzie

Jonathan

The three selected were Lizzie, John and Jonathan. I met them on the imposing stage of the Globe theatre, where they had one last hurdle to face – a final audition before Andy would make his recommendation to *Dr Who's* ultimate boss, Russell T. Davies.

All three acted their hearts out but in the end, Andy felt that there was a clear winner – 9-year-old John Bell from Kilmacolm in Scotland. Russell agreed wholeheartedly so the part was John's.

A few weeks after his audition, John reported to the *Dr Who* set in Cardiff for the all-important filming of his episode. John was playing the part of Creet, a refugee from the far distant future and his character was scheduled to appear in five important scenes to be shot over two days. Lizzie and Jonathan were there too, as they had been given non-speaking background parts as their runner-up prize.

Filming takes a long time and in the breaks John got to chat with everyone from the director to *Dr Who* stars David Tennant, Freema Agyeman and John Barrowman.

All the cast and crew admired John's instant professionalism. At the end of filming his final scene, everyone gave him a massive round of applause. David Tennant even picked him up and carried him on his shoulders for an impromptu victory march. John had done himself proud and now there was only the long wait until the finished episode was transmitted.

If you have stars in your eyes, like Piers and John, expect to work hard and be ready for tough competition. But if you've really got what it takes, you'll let nothing stand in your way. Good luck!

Andy

Andy Akinwolere

When I joined the team, the others told me I was about to begin a life full of never-to-be-forgotten moments. How right they were. A few weeks earlier, if you'd told me that I'd happily be putting on lots of make-up and dressing up in women's clothing, I'd never have believed you!

It was just before Christmas and Britain's most famous and successful pantomime dame, Christopher Biggins, had popped in to give me a lesson in being a lady. Chris is an old friend of Blue Peter and over the years he's helped many a supposedly butch Blue Peter presenter get in touch with their feminine side during panto season. I didn't want to be the first to break the tradition, so I reported to costume and make-up and let them loose on me. As they transformed me from Andy into Angela, I tried not to catch myself in the mirror. It was bad enough looking down and seeing my legs in those tights.

Men have played women in pantomimes for many years and back in Shakespeare's time, it was the law that all female parts had to be played by boys or men. Chris told me that in panto, the secret of a good cross-dressing comedy character is how they walk. He gave me a mini-masterclass and I did my best to follow his lead. I'm not sure what Magic made of it all though.

The item rushed by and before I knew it, it was time to take off my slap (that's what theatre people call their make-up), hang up my frock and surrender my wig. I can't actually say I was sorry but I'd had the best time giving it a go. I turned on my 'phone and there were a lot of texts from my mates – "Andy, u got gr8 legz" was one typical example. I could cope with the teasing. It was a small price to pay for a job where there's never a dull moment.

THAT'S SHOEBIZ!

Our ShoeBiz Appeal all started with one staggering fact. Two million pairs of shoes are thrown away every week in Britain. We thought there must be a way of turning those shoes into cash.

We knew what we wanted to spend the money on too. All over the world, countries are struggling to cope with the impact of a virus called HIV. HIV attacks the body's natural defences against disease and infection and if it isn't treated, people with the virus get extremely sick and develop AIDS. AIDS is still rare in Britain but in the developing world, it is killing millions and devastating many communities.

In Malawi in Africa, AIDS kills somebody every nine minutes. As a result, more than 600,000 children have lost one or both of their parents to AIDS. It is a tragedy on a massive scale. Imagine growing up without your Mum or Dad, often having to look after younger brothers and sisters too and even deal with bullying and exclusion because of what has happened to you. Some children have HIV themselves.

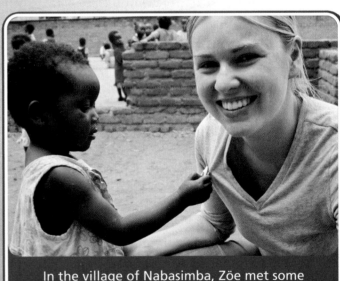

In the village of Nabasimba, Zöe met some children orphaned by AIDS: "They seem to be so content and happy just going about their activities and playing, and then you look into their eyes and there is an emptiness there. I'll never forget them as long as I live."

Working with our friends at the charity UNICEF, we wanted to pay for 22 Children's Corners. These are safe places where orphans can go for a meal, to make friends, remember their parents, take some basic lessons and most importantly of all, play and just have the chance to be children again.

Gethin took two typical Blue Peter viewers to Malawi to see a Children's Corner for themselves. Charlie is 12 and comes from London while Mica is 11 and lives in Liverpool. Charlie teamed up with Bon, who lost both his parents to AIDS. Charlie said later: "I got so attached to Bon, playing with him. He was different from what you would expect from somebody who has lost both his parents."

Mica made friends with Patricia. Mica said: "The children's corner really helps so if we can build more that will be really really cool because then there will be more happy children than sad."

Back in the studio, we unveiled our Totaliser. Our target was to collect 500,000 pairs of shoes – enough to pay for those 22 Children's Corners.

As ever, Blue Peter viewers rose to the challenge and shoes began to pour into our depot.
There they were sorted to be reconditioned and sold in the developing world.

Our good friend, gold badge winner David Beckham, donated his Real Madrid football boots, and lots of other celebrities followed his example, from pop stars Madonna and *X Factor*'s Leona to sporting heroes Amir Khan and Ryan Giggs and tv personalities like Jonathan Ross and Matt Willis, the winner of *I'm a Celebrity, Get Me Out of Here!*

The House of Commons even passed a motion supporting the ShoeBiz Appeal and the Prime Minister and MPs from all parties took a break from running the country to give us their shoes.

On January 16th, the flood of footwear meant we'd reached the 500,000 stage and although we were all delighted, we knew there was still so much we could do. We decided to set a brand-new target of one million pairs of shoes.

Just a few weeks later, on February 13th, the studio shook as our Totaliser shot out sparks and glitter. You'd done it! The one million stage was flashing away and that meant that, thanks to your efforts, we could double the help we were going to give thousands of orphans.

Andy flew back to Malawi for the opening of one of the children's corners Blue Peter viewers had paid for. It was a joyful occasion. All those shoes were already making a real difference to the lives of children who've had so much suffering and hardship to cope with. HIV and AIDS are far from beaten in Malawi or anywhere else, but the ShoeBiz Appeal showed how simple it is to do something to help. We'd like to say a massive thank-you to everyone who took part.

P.S. As we went to press on this book, the grand total of shoes collected had jumped another quarter of a million.

No Prizes for Gethin

Welsh cakes were one of my favourite tea-time treats when I was growing up and I still love them today. It was Konnie's idea to have a cook-off between Andy and me to see who could produce the tastiest version. The heat was on! Andy was obviously enjoying himself but I felt the pressure of flying the flag for Wales, not to mention my Auntie Jean, whose recipe we were using. Konnie tasted both our efforts and in the end, voted for Andy's. Funny that. Anyway, I still think he cheated by covering them with chocolate sauce! Now you can make a batch for yourself and see what you think...

INGREDIENTS

You'll need:

250g self-raising flour
130g butter
100g caster sugar
Seedless chopped raisins,
1 egg, beaten
Half a teaspoon of
baking powder
1 pinch of all spice
1 pinch salt
Tiny drop of milk

STAGE 1

Stir together the flour, the baking powder, the spice and the salt in a mixing bowl.

STAGE 2

Add the butter, chopped up, into your mixing bowl and rub into the flour until it resembles bread crumbs.

STAGE 3

Next mix in the sugar and the chopped raisins. Add the beaten egg and stir with a wooden spoon. If the mixture isn't sticking together, add a little milk. Don't make your mixture too sticky.

STAGE 4

Roll out on a lightly floured surface until the mixture is about 1cm thick. Cut out your cakes using a pastry cutter and cook for three minutes on each side using a greased griddle or heavy frying pan with the gas on a low setting.

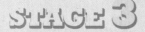

Sprinkle with sugar or add a favourite topping and then serve!

Going Dutch

I'd only just joined the team when I was told to pack my bags for my first overseas filming trip. Unfortunately, the airline we were travelling with managed to lose them so my first memories of our trip to Amsterdam in Holland are of the rush round the airport so that Geth and I could buy a few essentials before we started filming, like the T-shirts we've got on in this picture.

The Dutch are pretty laid-back people. Perhaps that's why a few years ago a game called pole-sitting was all the rage here. It is as simple as it sounds. You find a perch on one of the many wooden poles which jut out of the canal water and stay there as long as possible. Some people lasted days and so I challenged Geth to see how long he could make it. But after a very slow hour in the heat of the sun, we both decided to call it a day and agree on a draw.

There's a saying here, "God made the world but the Dutch made Holland", and you can see why it came about. Much of Holland's land is reclaimed from the sea and Amsterdam itself was built on water – there are hundreds of canals and bridges criss-crossing the city. The best way to experience it all is by boat, especially on a sunny afternoon.

Before the days of radios and recorded music, these street organs were the best way for people to enjoy popular tunes. The organs produce music just like the kind you hear coming from traditional funfair rides. This is one of the few that still remain in Amsterdam.

The traffic in the city is horrendous and most people get about by bicycle. In fact, there are more bikes here than people and you can hire one like we did very cheaply.

This is Geth and me all dressed up to have a go at Dutch folk-dancing – check out the clogs! We were trying to look cool but it was another incredibly hot day. When we go filming, we usually have just one camera and so it takes time to get all the shots you need to make up a story. We had to do our short dance over and over again and by the end, our clothes needed wringing out and I was glad I'd stocked up on deodorant at the airport. But I was beginning to get used to the bizarre demands of being a Blue Peter presenter.

While we were filming, we heard about a new kind of bike and after a few phone calls, managed to track down a couple to try out for ourselves. They're called segues and although they look simple enough, they're actually quite tricky to master. Filming this sequence took some time as we kept falling off, reversing or going off in completely the wrong direction.

Anne and her family were Jewish and back in 1940, when the Nazis occupied Amsterdam, that meant transportation to almost certain death in a concentration camp. Anne's father decided to hide his family and some friends in a secret apartment at the back of his firm's offices. The way in was hidden by this bookcase.

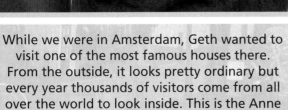

While we were in Amsterdam, Geth wanted to visit one of the most famous houses there. From the outside, it looks pretty ordinary but every year thousands of visitors come from all over the world to look inside. This is the Anne Frank house.

Only a very few people outside knew the secret. The family lived cramped together in a few small rooms, always in fear of discovery. This was Anne's bedroom, which she had to share. She pinned cuttings from magazines on the walls to make it more cheerful and you can still see them today.

Most importantly, Anne kept a diary in which she carefully recorded all her thoughts and feelings. She wrote:

'In the evenings it is the silence which frightens me so.'

They had stayed hidden for over two years now. But then, on August 4th 1944, the police burst in. The family and their friends had been betrayed. All of them were sent to concentration camps and only Anne's father Otto survived. Anne died just days before the end of the war.

The months went slowly by. Mr Frank kept a map charting the progress of the war and every day the family listened eagerly to the BBC news. Surely the war couldn't last for ever? By the summer of 1944, it was going badly for the Nazis and the hideaways began to hope.

By a miracle her diary survived and when it was published, it became an international sensation. In 1976, Mr Frank brought the diary to the Blue Peter studio.

Back in Amsterdam, Jacqueline van Maarsen, who was one of Anne's best friends, agreed to meet Geth in the park in front of Anne's home. She remembered Anne as lively, cheeky, "always wanting to be at the centre of things".

There's a statue of Anne in the park and Jacqueline said she felt sure that Anne would be delighted if she knew that she was remembered and thought about to this day. As Anne herself wrote: "'In spite of everything I still believe that people are really good at heart. If I look up into the heavens, I think that it will all come right, that this cruelty will end, and that peace and tranquillity will return again.'

Going Dutch

The idea is to launch yourself off a wooden runway, shin up your pole as fast as you can and land as far over on the other side of the canal as possible. Any miscalculation and the chances are you'll end up in the water, which is probably why canal-jumping competitions are popular with spectators.

The last filming day on our Going Dutch assignment involved a short drive out of the city into the flat, marshy countryside beyond. We were going 'up the pole', not a sequel to the pole-sitting we'd tried a few days before but a much older and more demanding Dutch sport – canal-jumping.

We actually did pretty well. I might be making a big splash in this photo but we both managed to jump the canal twice each. And anyway, being soaking wet in the summer sunshine was no hardship.

The whole trip had been great fun but for me the best thing about it was getting to know Geth and realising we were going to be good mates.

P.S. Our bags did turn up in the end!

Be Our Guest

This is a glimpse behind-the-scenes at Blue Peter, a shot of everyone working on the programme on the day we reached the one million stage on our ShoeBiz totaliser. It gave us the idea for this year's Annual competition. If you'd like an all-expenses paid trip to visit us and the pets at Television Centre in London, it really couldn't be easier to enter.

All we want you to do is tell us which of our pets are missing from the photo. When you think you've got the right answer, send it, together with your name, age, address and telephone number to:

BLUE PETER DAY OUT
BBC TELEVISION CENTRE
LONDON W12 7RJ

Entries must reach us by 28th February 2008 and the winner will be notified no later than 30th April 2008 when we'll agree a date for your V.I.P. visit. You can bring up to three other guests with you.

You'll also win one of our famous badges.

RULES: 1. Entrants must be under 15 and the competition is open to residents of the U.K, Ireland and the Channel Islands. 2. One winner will be chosen at random from the correct entries. 3. The judges' decision is final and no correspondence can be entered into. 4. Employees (and their relatives) of the BBC and Pedigree are not eligible to enter.

Nodding Dogs

If you love dogs as much as we do, how about making your very own four-legged friend? These ones are the spitting image of Mabel, Lucy and Magic and what's more they nod their heads too!

You'll need...

If you'd like to have a go, this is what you'll need: a small plastic water bottle, a washing liquid ball, thick and thin card, newspaper, diluted PVA glue, kitchen paper, coloured felt, short length of ribbon and some silver card, white and coloured paint (to match your dog), a drinking straw, a metal bolt and three nuts, a cocktail stick, a foam sheet.

Stage One

For the body, cover the bottle with a layer of papier mâché (strips of newspaper and diluted PVA glue). To get the shape of the front legs, roll two pieces of newspaper into sausage shapes. Roll one end up to form the foot and stick to one side of the bottle.

Stage Two

To shape the back legs, scrunch up some newspaper into a chicken drumstick shape, rolling the end up to form the foot and stick to both sides of the bottle, either side of the front legs. Stick strips of papier mâché over the legs to blend in with the rest of the body. Stick a length of string to the back of the bottle for the tail.

Stage Three

Cover the whole bottle with a layer of kitchen paper and diluted PVA glue to give a softer texture and leave to dry.

73

Time to move on to the head. This starts life as a plastic washing ball but you could cut out a section from a plastic ball instead. Cover the outside of the ball with a layer of papier mâché and then make the snout by rolling a piece of newspaper and glue into a ball and stick this to one side of the head. Cut two ear shapes in thin card and stick these to the head. Blend in the edges with strips of paper and glue. Cover with kitchen paper as before and leave to dry.

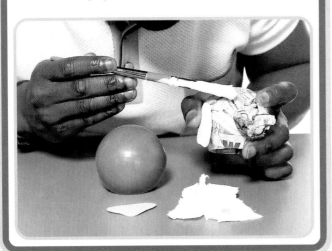

Paint the body and head with white emulsion paint and when dry, colour the body to match your dog with beige, black, white or brown. Cut out a triangular shape from black felt for the nose and two oval pieces of brown felt with black circles glued to the centre for eyes. Add a pink felt tongue under the nose. If you want to add a collar, just cut a length of ribbon to fit around the neck of the bottle just under the screw part. In the centre of the ribbon sew a tiny circle cut from silver card. Glue in place around the neck.

Now it is time to attach the head to the body. If you have a tool box at home, you might be lucky enough to find a bolt and three nuts, otherwise these only cost a few pence from a hardware shop. The bolt needs to fit inside a drinking straw. The nuts add weight to the pendulum which is what will make your dog's head nod. Screw the nuts onto the bolt and then push it into the straw or secure it with tape. Put the straw, with the weight at the bottom, into the body and then lift it up a little way from the base.

Keep holding it in that position while you make a hole with a pin level with the top of the bottle. Push a cocktail stick through the hole and cut both sides so that it just rests on top of the bottle.

Stage Eight

From a sheet of foam, cut one circle about 4cm in diameter and four smaller ones. Cut a small hole from the centre of the small circles. Glue the small circles together and then glue them on top of the larger one. Then glue this inside the head at the top.

Stage Nine

With the weighted straw inside the bottle, fit the other end of the straw into the hollow section of the foam inside the head. The head should then nod gently.

Stage Ten

For the base, cut two circles of thick card and stick them together. Neaten the edges by covering them with masking tape or paper and then paint. Stick your dog to the base.

As a finishing touch, find a small basket (the kind which often come with cosmetics) or make a mini dog-bed from a suitably sized cardboard box and some material. Your dog can then relax in complete comfort and whenever you want to give him or her the nod, just tap the back of the neck.

Gethin Jones

I've taken my life in my hands a few times on Blue Peter but none of those experiences have felt as frightening as the three days I spent undergoing the Royal Navy's submarine escape training. It is designed to help crews get safely out of a submarine if it becomes stranded on the seabed but it is not for the faint-hearted.

It all happens in this thirty-metre tank at Fort Blockhouse, *HMS Haslar* in Gosport. The crucial technique is to know exactly when you should hold your breath and when you shouldn't. Because of water pressure, the deeper you go, the more the volume of air in your lungs shrinks. When you come up again at a rate of six metres a second, it expands fast. Which means if you breathe in too soon or too quickly, your lungs can literally explode. Makes you think, eh?

Before I'd arrived, I'd been sent to the dentist. It was the same principle. Any gaps or cracks in my teeth able to trap air and as I ascended up the tank, they could explode. Makes you think even more! Happily, my teeth were given the OK. But if I didn't get my breathing timed correctly, I could still end up in real trouble. The advantage of an escape suit like this is that you can breathe normally all the way to the surface.

By the end of the three days, I'd ascended from nine and eighteen metres without a suit and from thirty metres with the suit on. Like anything, it got less scary with practice but danger is always a part of this exercise so I never relaxed my concentration. I was really pleased when I was told I'd passed. Now, in the unlikely event that I'm stuck in a stranded submarine, I'll feel a lot happier about my chances of survival. In the meantime, I was only too happy to be returning to dry land!

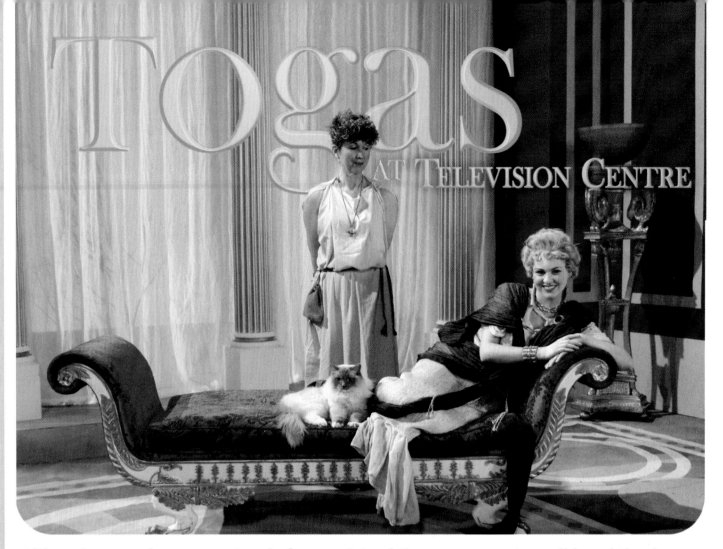

Togas AT TELEVISION CENTRE

Although none of us were actors before we joined the programme, we all loved the day we pretended to be Romans when our studio was transformed into a corner of ancient Rome. We discovered that there were some surprising similarities between their lives and ours.

Just like me, Roman ladies were very interested in fashion and beauty but I wasn't convinced by some of their favourite treatments. Here I am about to take a refreshing sip of my own urine. Romans believed it was a great mouthwash, helping to bleach the teeth whiter than white. I prefer toothpaste!

Guess who drew the short straw to play a slave? To Romans, slaves were an essential part of everyday life. They worked as anything from secretaries and accountants to cooks and child minders. They were bought and sold just as if they were household conveniences with prices matched to the skills or strengths they could offer. It was a hard life with terrible penalties if you dared to run away.

Meanwhile, I was trying to look manly and fierce as Gladiator Geth. Gladiator fighting was the top live entertainment of the time, a bit like big stadium sports events today. The difference is the players could end up dead! Gladiators underwent rigorous training and ate a high energy diet, exactly what I try to do to keep fit for my active life on Blue Peter.

The Romans were masters of fast food. Many Roman houses didn't have kitchens as they took up space and were a fire risk so stalls like mine did a roaring trade. Favourite dishes included lamb kebabs, chicken drumsticks and chickpea pancakes. Or you could have olives, roast nuts or fruit to eat on the go. There was even an early version of ice cream, made from fruit flavoured ice – delicious and refreshing. In many ways, the Romans were ahead of their time but, even so, none of us fancied a permanent life swap.

ALL TIED UP

Harry Houdini was the greatest escapologist the world has ever known. He risked his life performing ever more daring escapes in front of huge audiences. Nothing could hold him, not chains and padlocks, expertly tied ropes, police handcuffs or even tightly buckled strait-jackets, used to restrain prisoners and asylum patients. Although he died over 80 years ago, Houdini is still a celebrity today. When I told his story, I became so fascinated by the art of escapology that I decided to follow in his footsteps.

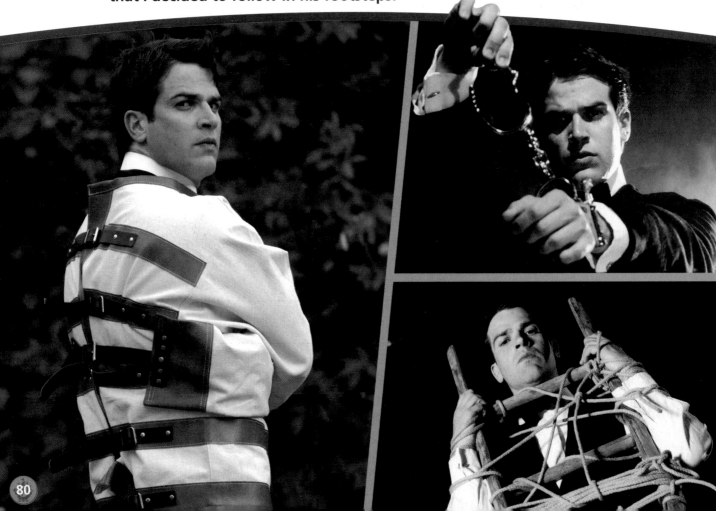

I was to perform my escape in front of a packed circus audience. In a matter of moments, I was all trussed up like a turkey at Christmas. I'd done a lot of practising but as Tom performed a final check to ensure that everything was tightly secured and that there was no trickery involved, I began to feel scared stiff.

I received expert instruction from one of Britain's best young escapologists, Tom Lyon, who has appeared on Blue Peter a few times over the years. He taught me some of the most important principles needed by a successful escape artist. These included using your flexibility to begin the process of loosening your bonds and most important of all, staying calm and focused. This is definitely not one to try at home.

As well as the rope and chains, I had to cope with being suspended upside down too. The blood rushed to my head as I began to twist and turn in the blaze of the bright lights. I felt sweat trickle down my back as I struggled to recall my training and concentrate on nothing but getting out. A couple of minutes later, I shook the last rope free. I felt a rush of adrenaline as the audience burst into applause and then I knew something of the thrill that the great Houdini must have felt throughout his spectacular career.

CAREFUL
WHAT YOU WISH FOR...

…or it just may come true! That's a saying that perhaps Konnie and I should have remembered before we got the wise idea of suggesting a challenge ourselves. We'd been chatting about how whether we could survive being stranded and having to live off the land. We mentioned the idea in passing to the Editor of Blue Peter and we were surprised by how enthusiastic he seemed. "Great idea, let's do it. Soon." "Why the rush?" I asked. "Before you have time to have second thoughts," he replied, as if second thoughts were inevitable, adding, "Remember – be careful what you wish for…"

A few days later, it was all fixed. We had a couple of days' survival training from expert Paul Johnson but we were told nothing about our destination. That was part of the challenge. "Oh Zo, just think, we might end up on a little island somewhere in the Caribbean," Konnie whispered dreamily to me. "Endless white sand, deep blue sea and fabulous tropical fruits to feast on."

The reality turned out to be rather different.

We ended up on the Isle of Mull, just off the coast of Scotland. We were dropped off by the local RNLI and left to it. It was a bitterly cold February so Konnie's tropical daydreams were soon forgotten as we concentrated on our priorities – finding shelter and food.

The big problem turned out to be keeping a fire going. We just couldn't seem to master it and with no fire, there was no food and no heat either. Our luxury items – a hot water bottle each – were useless. As I hate the cold more than anything else, it was totally miserable. We had very little sleep on that first night and it wasn't until we mastered the fire and how to keep it going that things got better.

Once we'd shooed away a stray goat, we found a good, dry cave. Food was more of a problem. First we collected some mussels, which we'd have to wash and then boil. Then we came across a dead deer, which had been killed by keepers to control the local deer population and protect the range of wildlife here. It would be a great source of meat, if we could remember our training and overcome our squeamishness to skin it and cut it up. Hunger won the day. It really made us think how much we take our food supply for granted and how little we think about where our meat comes from.

Mull is a beautiful, peaceful place but would we honestly miss it? As we began the long journey home, back to hot and cold running water, ready meals and technology, we thought about what we'd got out of our experience. We both had a sense of pride that we'd coped and got through it. We'd had time to talk and enjoy our friendship, with no distractions. We'd had time to wonder at the beauty of nature and realise how protected we are from it in our busy modern lives. That saying came back to me. Be careful what you wish for, it might just come true. When it does, it can leave you with a lot to think about.

Our second night was much more successful. We cooked our venison (Konnie had smuggled in some tomato ketchup to go with it) and were completely cosy in our cave. Next morning, just as we'd set out to fish for our next meal, we caught sight of the RNLI boat on the horizon. We were being rescued! Paul was on the boat, smiling from ear to ear. "You survived!" he grinned, "How good do you feel? Want to stay a few more nights?"

We both scrambled hurriedly into the boat.

Blue Peter ON ICE

I'd only been learning to drive for a couple of months when I was told I was going to be sent somewhere where my skills would be pushed to a whole new level. Jukkasjarvi in Sweden is two hundred kilometres north of the Arctic Circle. World class rally drivers come here to perfect their driving style on Sweden's frozen lakes. I was a long way from that kind of standard but I hoped I might brush up on the basics of my steering and stopping.

I soon discovered that ice driving is a fantastic way of getting to grips with your motor skills. Just like my ordinary lessons, I had a co-driver at all times who could easily take over if I lost control. I did a lot of slipping and sliding but managed to stay in charge of the steering wheel. Driving in these conditions in Britain is highly dangerous but here I could practise as much as I liked, knowing there was nothing close by to crash into.

After an excellent lesson, Konnie joined me for a skidoo race, a very different feeling from driving a car.

Konnie and I shot around the course with our skidoos spraying up clouds of snow. It was completely exhilarating to speed through the sparkling white landscape.

Inside, the beds are made from solid blocks of ice, covered with thick reindeer skins. Konnie thought it felt like walking into the land of Narnia. She was as enchanted as I was. I'd been told that a dip in the hot tub here was a great way to unwind after a hard day's driving and when I suggested it to Konnie, she thought it was a great idea.

This was our hotel. The ice hotel. Every winter, artists from all over the world gather to carve this magnificent temporary structure from the frozen waters of the nearby River Torne. It takes 30,000 square metres of snow and 4000 tonnes of ice to complete the job and every spring all that hard work just melts away again.

The only snag is that the hotel insist that to feel the full benefit of the bubbling warm water, first you have to plunge into this icy outdoor pool of water. The air temperature was an invigorating minus 38 degrees so we didn't waste too much time stripping off our dressing gowns and getting on with it.

The agony over and it was into the hot tub. This was more like it! I went over all the tips I'd picked up from my sub-zero motor masterclass. In a few weeks time, I'd be hoping to pass my driving test first time. When I'd started lessons back in London, I certainly had no idea they'd end up leading me to a super-cool adventure in a real-life winter wonderland.

P.S. – Andy passed his test with flying colours!

85

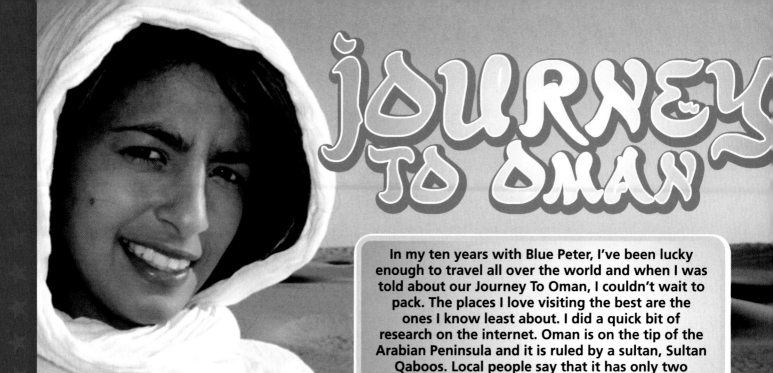

JOURNEY TO OMAN

In my ten years with Blue Peter, I've been lucky enough to travel all over the world and when I was told about our Journey To Oman, I couldn't wait to pack. The places I love visiting the best are the ones I know least about. I did a quick bit of research on the internet. Oman is on the tip of the Arabian Peninsula and it is ruled by a sultan, Sultan Qaboos. Local people say that it has only two seasons – 'hot summer' and 'pleasant summer'. It is a world apart in so many ways and yet it is only about eight hours by plane from the UK.

Most people in Oman are Muslim and follow the religion of Islam. We'd arrived at the end of the holy month of Ramadan, when Muslims fast in daylight hours, and just before the massive three-day Eid celebrations, when everyone visits friends and family. A new outfit for Eid is a must and Andy and I decided to shop for ours. This was Andy's choice. A lot of the men in Oman wear outfits like this – it's called a dishdashas and the hat is a kummah. I thought Andy looked great and he told me it was really cool and comfortable to wear.

But not everything is so traditional here. Freestyling or 'B-Boying' is the latest dance craze. Until just a few years ago, this kind of dancing was frowned upon. Slowly people have come round to it, won over by the enthusiasm and skill of the young boys who practise it in their every spare moment and who argue it is a real discipline for their mind, body and spirit.

Camel-racing is big business. Racing camels can change hands for as much as 75,000 Rial, about £100,000. As a result, it is not surprising that camels are often treated like kings, fed on a diet of alfalfa plants and dates, washed down with bottles of ghee (a kind of butter mixed with water).

After Andy had met the boys, I showed him the outfit I'd found for myself. The long black dress is called an abaya and almost all the women we met in Oman wear one. Camels are Oman's number one animal, not just for transport or meat or even their milk but for entertainment.

I met Saeed who owns 25 camels which he breeds for racing. Saeed let me help with their daily grooming regime. I've washed a few animals in my time on the programme but shampooing a camel in the Omani desert must count as one of the strangest examples.

Saeed suggested that Andy and I should have a go at camel-riding. Before we knew it, we were processing gracefully along the sand dunes. It was a wonderful experience and although I didn't quite feel ready to enter a race, I could see exactly why the Omanis love their camels so much.

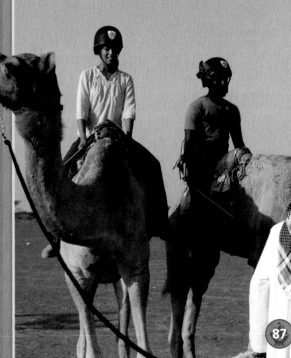

Everywhere we went in Oman, we were given a warm welcome. With Eid just around the corner, many people were busy planning feasts. We met 13-year-old Qais, who told us about the special treat enjoyed by his village. It is a unique meal called a Shuwa and it is contained inside this sack. But Qais told us that there were more to be prepared and that we could help.

Qais sent Andy off to find an armload of banana leaves and some spices. Fresh goat meat is carefully marinated with these spices, wrapped in the banana leaves and put inside the sack. Every family in the village follows the same method and all the Shuwa sacks are cooked together for three days in an underground pit covered with date palm leaves.

The Shuwa is eaten for breakfast or lunch on the third day of Eid and we joined the village party to taste it for ourselves. The ultra-slow cooking process makes the meat incredibly tender and very delicious. Everyone was in high spirits. I tried to explain that we often cook on Blue Peter but we certainly don't have three days to get our recipes just right!

Not far from the village, I had another warm welcome from Seyad the Snake Man. There are 32 different kinds of snake in Oman, of which ten are venomous. Seyad has spent 15 years collecting and documenting them. He often takes snakes into schools to try to show children that, once you know your stuff, snakes are nothing to be scared of. He asked if I'd like a demonstration myself and this was the result. I wasn't worried. Well, maybe a bit.

The Hajar mountains are an awesome sight, famous for their massive cliffs and gorges. Andy was quite happy taking in the views but he suggested I take up the challenge of getting a bird's eye view of the amazing scenery.

Seyad would have approved as this is the Snake Gorge. It is one of the best-known and my journey across it was by zip wire. Unlike Andy, I'm not too frightened by heights but I'm not careless either and the concentration needed meant I couldn't really stop to enjoy the view after all.

We finished our journey in Oman's Wahiba sands, staying in the desert home of a Bedouin nomad called Shaikah. The Bedouin live in tents, grazing their animals and moving on when either food or water get scarce. Shaikah wears a mask to protect her modesty from strangers and her face from the harsh sun. After a dinner of shark meat, I looked up into the stars shining over the endless, shifting sands, thought how little I'd known about Oman before and remembered that there are so many wonderful places out there just waiting to be explored.

Rule Britannia!

The royal yacht Britannia is a very special ship. For over four decades she carried the Queen and her family on state business all over the world, sailing many millions of miles. As well as allowing Her Majesty to entertain VIPs, kings, queens and heads of state, Britannia was also used for royal holidays and honeymoons.

I went on board as a "yottie" or royal yachtsman, one of the sailors who kept the ship constantly gleaming. It was a great honour to join the crew.

But it was certainly very hard work too. First thing every morning, the decks had to be scrubbed down with pails of water. No shouting was allowed on board ship so orders were often given using hand signals.

At sea, every flag has a meaning and on board Britannia I found the Blue Peter, the flag which is hoisted to indicate that a ship is about to set sail on her next voyage. It was this flag which gave our programme its name.

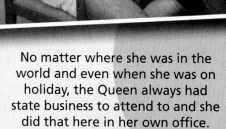

Britannia was a combination of floating royal palace and working ship. This is the Queen's drawing room, where she received important visitors. Originally she wanted a real coal fire here but when she was told that this would mean a sailor standing by at all times with a bucket of water in case of fire, she settled for electric instead.

No matter where she was in the world and even when she was on holiday, the Queen always had state business to attend to and she did that here in her own office.

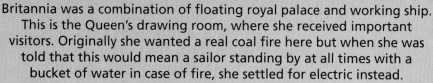

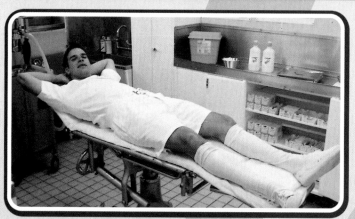

The ship's designers seemed to think of everything. I was amazed to discover that Britannia actually had its own operating theatre, in case of any serious injuries or accidents.

The ship is full of surprises. Hidden away inside one of the funnels I even found a tiny gym, where the sailors could keep fit.

When she was finally decommissioned or retired in 1997, Britannia was fully restored and opened to the public as a fascinating floating museum. If you are a Blue Peter badge-winner you can explore it free.

White uniforms look smart but they get dirty easily and sailors often had to change several times a day. No wonder there is a huge laundry on board. In an emergency, Britannia could be transformed into a hospital ship with the laundry standing in as a ward. Luckily, it never needed to.

A Victorian Christmas

You are invited to spend Christmas with the Jones family, who lived in a typical, wealthy Victorian home...

Back then, Christmas was only just starting to become the celebration we know and love today. Christmas cards, for instance, were a new idea and they took off because cheap postage was introduced and the ever-growing railway network could carry the cards all over Britain. Mrs Jones was delighted to receive a card from a dear family friend, Mr Baker. "And doing so well with his missionary work," she beamed merrily.

The work in a wealthy Victorian household was done by the servants. They had to grab their fun in between the never-ending jobs they had to do. Crackers were another new invention. A Victorian sweet-maker called Tom Smith had been sitting next to his fireside when it let off a loud crack. This gave Smith the inspiration to put the all-important bang in his crackers. Constance and Andrew, the Jones's faithful servants, were taking a big risk trying one out. If they were caught, they might have been sacked on the spot and no-one else would have given them another job, Christmas or not. It was Constance's idea, of course. "All this for them upstairs," she said. "They'll not miss one measly cracker." As Andrew remarked, that Constance always was a saucy minx.

Meanwhile, Mr Jones, the Master of the House, had arranged a special seasonal surprise for his excited wife. A visit from Father Christmas! Her excitement quickly faded when she realised it was just Collins the gardener, dressed up and treading mud into her expensive rug. Mr Jones sent him back to the hothouse sharpish. By the way, don't be confused by the colour of Father Christmas's suit – the now-famous red outfit didn't make its first appearance for decades to come.

The Christmas tree was introduced to Britain by Queen Victoria's husband, Prince Albert. It was a tradition in Germany, where he came from. But they could be dangerous back in the nineteenth century. Real candles meant a big fire risk so that a servant often had to stand by with a bucket of water in case the tree caught fire.

In Victorian times, children only got one Christmas present and it wasn't wrapped. Nothing was mass-produced, so all toys were hand-made. This made them very expensive, so only well-off children got to play with them. The Jones children were luckier than most but they were expected to behave themselves at all times and had to wear fussy and often uncomfortable clothes.

Because there were no films, tv, dvds, computers, console games or recorded music, families had to entertain themselves. Carol-singing was a highlight and each Christmas, the poor children of a neighbourhood would walk around the area, singing for food and money. Mince pies were often handed out as a reward for their efforts, though the loudest singer in the Jones household was always Mrs Jones. "We wish you a Merry Christmas", she trilled happily, ignoring the children's giggles.

Just like today, the high point of the day was the big meal. The whole family would gather round the table to enjoy the food, company and spirit of Christmas. Turkey was the main dish but only if you could afford it. Poorer families had to make do with rabbit. Mrs Jones wondered if her idea of having turtle soup to start was too much for Cook to manage.

Cooks certainly had their work cut out for them. Christmas dinner often meant five or six courses with treats like raw oysters, quail, candied fruit and plum pudding. All this meant a lot of clearing away and washing up for the servants who laboured long into the night 'below stairs' so that the family 'upstairs' could enjoy themselves. "Just a few more trays to go," smiled Andrew. "I'll not see my bed till Boxing Day," muttered Constance bitterly. Her hands were already red raw.

Games like blind man's buff offered a rare chance for children from rich households to spend time with their parents. Usually they saw very little of them as they were looked after by nannies and nursery maids. Boys were sent away to boarding school at the age of seven while girls usually had a governess.

Servants like Andrew and Constance very rarely had real holidays or proper time off. But there were some perks – presents from the Master and Mistress (usually something useful like material to make themselves new clothes) and a chance to have their own Christmas meal, with beer and wine provided. "Happy Christmas, Constance," smiled Andrew. "Get that mince pie eaten before Cook notices you're having a sit down!"

This might seem harsh but servants actually had a much better quality of life than most other poor or working people. They had hot food and a roof over their heads and they knew that however long the hours and boring the work, there were plenty of people far worse off – not just at Christmas but all year round.

A late-night ghost story was a favourite Christmas treat and it was during Victorian times that some of the best-ever ghost stories were written. While Mr Jones threw himself into the terror of his tale, Mrs Jones tried not to think too hard about phantoms and instead kept her mind on what she would tell Cook about the turtle soup, which had not been a success. Christmas was just about over for another year.

We all found our trip back in time fascinating but one thing is certain. A Victorian Christmas was a lot more fun if you were rich enough to afford it.

Zöe

Zöe Salmon

Ever since I was little, I've loved dancing and performing and when I joined Blue Peter, I hoped there would be plenty of both. I can't say I've been disappointed. There was my ice dancing challenge, the week I joined the *Royal Variety Show* as a dancer, our history of duets, not to mention our Christmas spectacular.

When the call came for me to become one of the contestants in this year's *Comic Relief Fame Academy,* I was flattered and terrified at the same time. I don't know what made me blurt out that I rated my singing talent as seven out of ten. What I meant was that I'd like to get to that level. But there was no time to kick myself. There were songs to learn and choreography to master. In the end, I was delighted I lasted four shows, though stepping into the circle of fear, as the stage was called, was never less than terrifying.

Riverdancing has helped bring the magic of Irish dance to audiences all over the world. Like so many dance styles, it looks much easier than it really is. To produce the right result, all the performers have to dance as one, with perfect timing and particular control of their upper bodies. I joined the cast after a few days rehearsal for what we hoped would be a dazzling special performance in the Blue Peter studio. I'd never done any Irish dancing as a child and getting this right really meant the world to me. It went fantastically well and the second we finished, the applause rang out. I felt my heart beating, my skin glowing and a smile I couldn't stop. What an incredible feeling. Now I just wanted to do it all over again.

Monster Masks

Scare your friends and family with one of these gruesome masks, perfect for anyone planning a party or play with a Dr Who or Halloween theme. You can take your pick from evil green, silver robot or wicked witch.

Essential Ingredients

Believe it or not, all the masks start life as a detergent bottle with a long handle. Your other essential ingredients are: tissue paper, a ping-pong ball, wobbly eyes, a sheet of coloured plastic foam, paint and some raffia, string or wool for hair.

Stage One

First, cut the screw top from the top of the bottle. Using small scissors, carefully cut down the centre back and around the base. Round off the corners and make the hole larger at the top.

Stage Two

Hold the mask up to your face and place your finger on the outside in line with your eye. Mark with a pen then draw a semi-circle. Cut out two eye-holes and a mouth-shape just behind the nose.

Stage Three

To help the paint stick to the plastic bottle, first cover it with with pieces of tissue paper, which you stick all over the bottle using diluted PVA glue. The tissue paper will wrinkle, which is the effect you want. Leave this to dry for a couple of hours and then start painting. Choose a sludgy brown or fluorescent green for a gruesome effect and give a darker shade around the eye sockets and mouth.

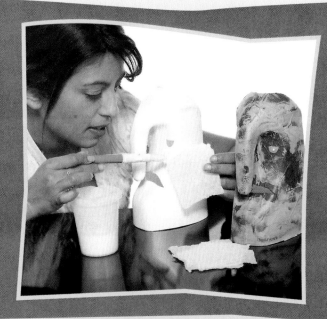

Monster Masks

Stage Four

While the paint is drying, make the eyes. You could just paint in a semi-circle on top of the cut-out holes and then stick on a wobbly eye. To make some goggly eyes using a ping-pong ball, cut the ping-pong ball in half and paint to match or contrast with the main face. Then glue a large wobbly eye on top.

Stage Five

To attach the eyes to the mask, cut a narrow strip of plastic or card. Tape one end inside the eye. Push the other end through the eye-hole and tape to the inside of the mask. Make sure it doesn't completely cover the eye-hole.

Stage Six

The ears are just shapes cut from a sheet of plasticised foam with an extra tab on one side. When you have decided where you want your ears to go, cut a slit in each side of the mask the same size as the tab. Push the tab through the mask and tape on the inside to secure the ear.

Stage Seven

For the hair, cut some lengths of raffia or string and glue them to the top of the mask on the inside.

Stage Eight

Finally, make a hole each side of the back of the mask and thread some elastic through, making a knot on the inside each side.

The Silver Robot

For the silver robot stick some bubble wrap on the sides and chin and across the bottle under the nose. Cut out a wide mouth. Glue three strands of wool on the forehead in a wavy style. The ears are two mini yoghurt pots stuck on each side of the head. Paint the whole mask silver. As a finishing touch, stick some strands of silver gift ribbon on the chin and glue some card teeth inside the mouth.

The Witch

If you prefer a wicked witch, make the mask as before but then roll up tissue paper to create witchy warts and a longer, pointed chin. Paint your mask a fleshy colour with a tinge of green. Use a dark shade round the eye-holes and red round the mouth. Stick your wobbly eyes above the eye-holes and make the hair from green raffia or wool.

Once you've made your mask, you're all ready to scare the living daylights out of your unlucky victims...

HAVE A GO GETH

Olympic freestyle wrestling is one of the oldest sports around. Men have been trying their strength and unarmed skill against each other since the dawn of time and now it was my turn to have a go. I was trained to take part in a novice tournament at Edinburgh's Heriot-Watt University.

The rules of wrestling are very precise. The aim is to pin your opponent on the mat. Along the way there are all kinds of different moves you can use to score points and take out your opponent. These moves have names like "leg attack" and "head snap", which gives you some idea of how much they can hurt. You need strength, flexibility and speed to have any chance of being good.

My opponent was a slim, wiry Scot called Davy, who has been wrestling since he was six years old. Davy didn't waste time on pleasantries like hellos and handshakes. He just sized me up,

like a cobra checking out his breakfast. I tried to make a joke about the kit wrestlers have to wear but he was having none of it.

It was time to get down to business, a Celtic confrontation between Scotland and Wales. I thought a bit of mind over matter might help so I concentrated on transforming myself into Bonecrusher Jones. But when you're in the hands of an experienced wrestler like Davy, defeat is only a matter of time and how much pain you go through to get there. I didn't give in easily but it was all over soon enough.

I had managed to avoid total humiliation but nobody was surprised when the referee lifted the victorious Davy's arm in the air. My trainer, Olympic coach Michael Cavanagh, told me I'd done very well for a beginner. I ached all over but praise from a top professional meant a lot.

We were given some training and a lot of inspiration from fellow Welshman, gold-badge winning and undefeated world champion Joe Calzaghe. Joe sparred with both of us to assess our skill and chances. As it was quickly obvious that neither Matt nor I had much in the way of experience, Joe reckoned it would be a fair contest.

Boxing has been around almost as long as wrestling. Today it causes many arguments because of the violence involved but for me it was a case of unfinished business. I'd already had a bruising encounter with the sport the year before when a training session with rising boxer Kevin Mitchell ended with me throwing up and paramedics being called in. At the time, I was upset and annoyed and felt I could do much better given the chance. This was it. The idea was that I'd train to fight an old Cardiff-based friend of mine, Matt Johnson, in an amateur boxing contest.

HAVE A GO GETH

But then disaster struck. All amateur boxing matches are strictly controlled for maximum safety and before we could fight, both of us had to pass a medical. Matt sailed through his but my poor eyesight was my undoing. Because there was an increased risk that I could detach a retina, I was refused permission to continue. Frustrated, disappointed, angry, sad. All words that can't quite sum up how bad I felt about it. When Matt said he still wanted to go ahead and fight, I decided to turn my energies into supporting him instead.

A couple of weeks later, Matt squared up against a local lad called Wayne. Three hard rounds later and Wayne was declared the winner. To me, Matt was the real hero of the day. Bruised, battered and bloody though he was, he'd never faltered. Looking back, it is hard to say what I really feel about boxing. At its best, it is a great sport to watch and it takes incredible bravery to step inside the ring. But it can be very brutal too and as I looked at my mate's swollen, damaged face, I wondered how I'd have felt if that had been my fault or if I'd got the same treatment from him.

We threw ourselves into the training. Matt told me: "My dad boxed as a young man and I've always been fascinated by boxing." We talked a lot about how weird it was to be working towards a fight where we'd both deliberately set out to hit and hurt each other. I couldn't quite get my head round it, though Matt said he'd have no problems punching me!

My next opponent wasn't human but cold steel. In weightlifting, it is just you and the bar. As I found out, it is very addictive and in the end all you want to do is push yourself to lift more. Just like wrestling and boxing, weightlifting has been around for thousands of years.

My coach, ex-weightlifting champion Keith Morgan, taught me the basics of the two lifts used in competitive weightlifting – the snatch and the clean and jerk. We started off using a broom handle so I got my technique just right. You can do serious damage to yourself if you don't.

To stand any chance in a competition, you have to be able to lift at least your own body weight. In my case, that's about 80kg and believe me, it takes some doing. Your muscles burn, your breath is sucked out of your body and your face twists into a mask of pure effort. By now, though, I was used to the pain. Then, at last, I had lift-off and what's more I'd managed it without an injury in sight. Happy days!

The months I spent working on my *Have a Go Geth* series have been among the most demanding and rewarding of my life so far. They've given me a chance to understand from the inside why different sports inspire so much passion and commitment. I can't wait to get into training for some more.

HAPPY ONE HUNDREDTH!

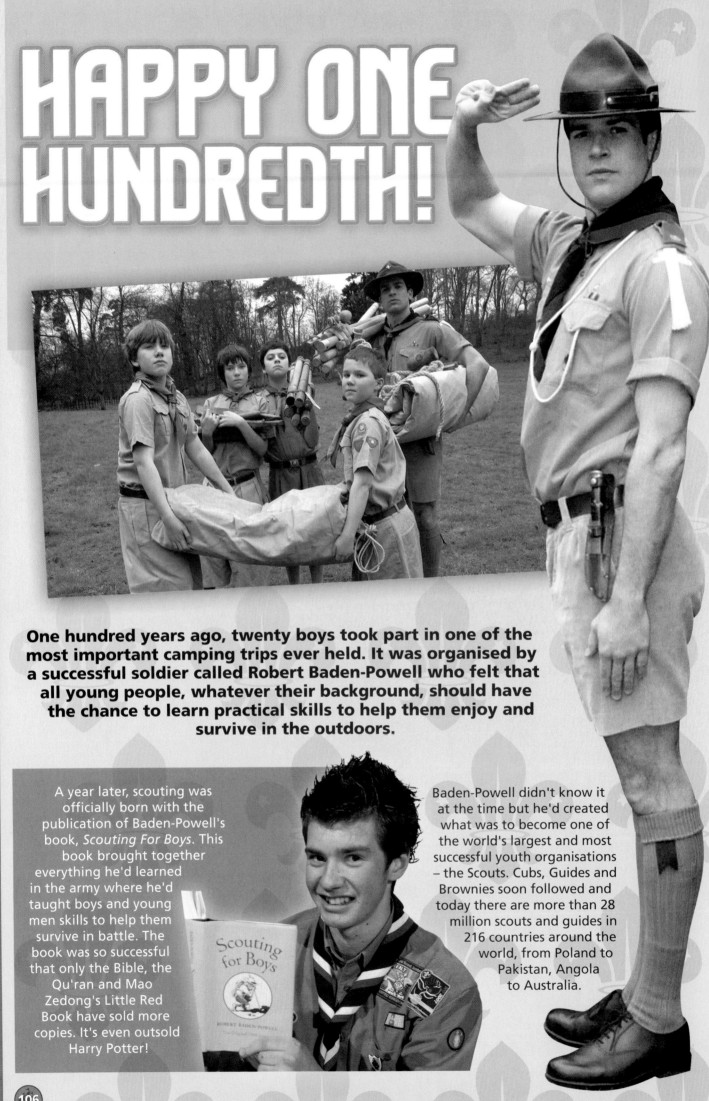

One hundred years ago, twenty boys took part in one of the most important camping trips ever held. It was organised by a successful soldier called Robert Baden-Powell who felt that all young people, whatever their background, should have the chance to learn practical skills to help them enjoy and survive in the outdoors.

A year later, scouting was officially born with the publication of Baden-Powell's book, *Scouting For Boys*. This book brought together everything he'd learned in the army where he'd taught boys and young men skills to help them survive in battle. The book was so successful that only the Bible, the Qu'ran and Mao Zedong's Little Red Book have sold more copies. It's even outsold Harry Potter!

Baden-Powell didn't know it at the time but he'd created what was to become one of the world's largest and most successful youth organisations – the Scouts. Cubs, Guides and Brownies soon followed and today there are more than 28 million scouts and guides in 216 countries around the world, from Poland to Pakistan, Angola to Australia.

It's not every day you get to celebrate a hundredth birthday and we thought this one was worthy of a massive party. There were a lot of guests for a start, with 120 scouts from all over Britain cramming into our studio. And, as you would expect, there was a magnificent cake to mark the special occasion.

Even Mabel, Lucy, Magic and Socks joined in the fun and were given their own honorary scout scarves to wear.

We thought it would be a good idea to set a true scouting challenge – a race between two teams to see which could put up their tent in our garden and raise their flag the fastest. The teams were captained by Zöe and ex-Blue Peter presenter and Chief Scout, Peter Duncan, who has come a long way since he too was a cub scout!

The whistle went and the competition was intense. To make things more interesting, we even provided some authentic bad camping weather conditions! Neither side had any intention of losing. But of course there could only be one winner and in the end, it was Peter's team who triumphed.

HAPPY ONE HUNDREDTH!

That was just the warm-up, however. Together with our friends at the Guinness Book of Records, we decided to "do our best" to set a world record live in the studio. As it was Pancake Day, we thought a pancake tossing record would be just right and there was the added bonus that we could scoff the end result, whether we set the record or not!

To be in with a chance, the rules stated that the maximum number of people needed to keep tossing the same pancake continuously for 30 seconds. The Guinness officials had their stopwatches at the ready and there were independent adjudicators to ensure fair play too. As the seconds to the record attempt counted down, you could feel the tension running throughout the studio. Everyone wanted to nail it. Next thing we knew, the air was full of high-flying pancakes. It was mayhem. There were a few casualties of course, pancakes which ended up a soggy mess on our studio floor.

But we did it – and the world pancake-tossing record now stands at 108.

Right at the end of the programme we surprised our old mate Peter Duncan by awarding him with our highest honour, the gold Blue Peter badge. We thought that he'd earned it after five years as a Blue Peter presenter and now his job as Britain's Chief Scout. Just for once, Pete was speechless!

It had been a brilliant birthday party.

Scouts have come a long way in the last century. There have been many changes, from the uniforms worn and the badges won to the actual activities themselves. But despite all these changes, every scout still follows the basic rules laid down by Baden-Powell all those years ago – to do their best and to be prepared.

Solutions & Credits

Get in touch at:
Blue Peter
BBC TV Centre
London W12 7RJ

or email: bluepeter@bbc.co.uk

bbc.co.uk/cbbc/bluepeter

Written by Richard Marson
Photography by Chris Capstick
Illustrations by Bob Broomfield
Makes by Gillian Shearing
Food by Diggy Hicks-Little

Other photographs by Andy Akinwolere,
Benjamin Cook, Andy Clarke, Crown Copyright,
Tim Fransham, Darren Harbar, Gethin Jones,
Richard Kendal, Marc Hill, Adrian Homeshaw, Mike Lawn,
Kate Lukeman, Richard Marson, Debbie Martin,
Kara Miller, Rob Norman, Thomas Orger, Sue Osmond,
Adrian Rogers, Ros Sewell, David Graeme-Baker, Paul Stas,
Beth Thomas, Richard Turley, Ed Willson

Bash Street Kids © + ® DC Thomson and Co Ltd. 2007

The author would like to thank Bridget Caldwell,
Melissa Hardinge, Jack Lundie, Audrey Neil and the
Blue Peter team for their help and ideas. Every effort has
been made to contact copyright holders for permission
to reproduce material in this book. If any material has
been used without permission, please contact us.

Wayne's in Pain

This was the winning design in our Bash Street Kid competition. Seven-year-old James Thompson won with Wayne's In Pain, who constantly hurts himself and is always covered in cuts and bruises. The judges loved the comedy potential of Wayne, the first new continuing character to join the Bash Street gang in 25 years.

HELLO THERE! PICTURE SOLUTIONS

1) Top cricketer and *Strictly Come Dancing* champion Mark Ramprakash put on his whites and joined us in the studio to test a brand-new virtual cricket helmet and an automated bowling machine.

2) We took a train trip back in time on board the fabulously elegant Orient Express, the most stylish way to travel across Europe in the 1920s and 30s. Konnie was the glamorous but demanding passenger, while Gethin did his best to provide good service.

3) What happens if you get stuck in a cable car, hundreds of metres above the Derbyshire countryside? You hope for expert rescue and Zöe learnt exactly what that requires when she joined the team in charge in case of emergency.

4) More famous faces, this time the Scooby Doo gang who got all of us involved in our own mini-episode, *The Mystery of the Missing Badges*. It turned out that Zelda, Zöe's so far unheard-of evil twin sister, had done it. And she would have gotten away with it if it hadn't been for those meddling Blue Peter presenters!

5) Thriller was the biggest selling album of all time. Andy stunned the studio with his precision dancing when he took the lead role in a one-off performance from the touring version.

6) Top film star, gold badge winner and good friend of the programme, Ewan McGregor, came to the studio to talk about his visit to Malawi and to take a close look at some priceless original examples of work by Beatrix Potter. Ewan had just appeared in a film playing Beatrix's publisher.

7) Konnie travelled to Old Trafford to award another gold badge, this time to Wayne Rooney, one of Britain's best footballers.

8) Zöe was back trying anything once when she took to the skies as a wing walker. As well as an incredible experience in its own right, it had special significance for Zöe. One of her earliest Blue Peter memories was seeing presenter Caron Keating, who was also from Northern Ireland, tackle the same daredevil assignment.

9) The Blue Peter boys threw themselves into the sticky game of swamp soccer. The teams have very suitable names. Andy played for Dirtdee United while Geth joined Real Mudrid. Despite the constant hazards of getting stuck and falling over, Andy scored a hatric, helping his side to win 4-3.

10) As the Harry Potter saga came to its magical conclusion, author J.K. Rowling visited the Blue Peter studio for a special programme. She was another famous face who we thought well deserved our highest honour, a gold badge.

11) Geth in Venice, trying his skill as a Gondolier. This was taken moments before he lost his balance and plunged into the murky waters of the Grand Canal.